To Andrew

We're glad you were part of BB+N in 1991!

With love + good wishes,

Rosalie + Rosi

BOSTON

BOSTON

FRANK FOSTER
&
JOHN D. SPOONER

SKYLINE PRESS

Produced by Boulton Publishing Services, Inc., Toronto
Designed by Fortunato Aglialoro

©1986 Oxford University Press (Canadian Branch)
SKYLINE PRESS is a registered imprint of the Oxford University Press

ISBN 0-19-540620-6
1 2 3 4 – 9 8 7 6
Printed in Hong Kong by Scanner Art Services, Inc., Toronto

Introduction

Bostonians like to believe what Oliver Wendell Holmes said, that 'Boston's State House is the hub of the solar system. You couldn't pry that out of a Boston man, if you had the tire of all creation straightened out for a crow bar.' In many ways, Boston still thinks of herself as the hub of the universe. There was a dinner party held in Louisburg Square, in the heart of Beacon Hill. A young woman, recently married, was approached by an old Boston dowager, a grande dame with imposing bosom and equally imposing jewelry. Seeing an unfamiliar face the older woman questioned the newlywed with a traditional Boston greeting. 'Where are you from, my dear?'

Without hesitation, though slightly defensive, the young woman answered, 'I'm from Iowa.'

The grande dame looked at her sharply. 'In Boston,' she said imperiously, 'we pronounce it *Ohio*.' Many things have changed in Boston since this dowager was a débutante. Strangers are no longer sniffed around; it doesn't take three generations to gain acceptance to the finest homes, country clubs and eating societies. Indeed the key to understanding this historic American city, now in its 355th year, is in its contrasts, its blending of the traditional and the modern. You see the antique brick sidewalks, the glass and steel skyscrapers, the Brahmin bankers in their vests and gold watch-chains, the young high-technology wizards in their designer jeans. But you must start your understanding of Boston with a feeling for the history that underlies all of these seeming contradictions.

You can begin your introduction in the lobby of the Bank of New England, in the midst of the financial district. A mural fills the north wall of the bank. It is an oil painting of the Boston Massacre, which occurred on 5 March 1770. It is done in blood reds and colonial blues and it jumps out at small depositors and major borrowers alike as they enter the ground floor. But the painting is not what you would expect, a representational study of history, on loan from a museum. It is rather a special commission done by the modern American painter Larry Rivers. The British 'lobster-backs' line up in efficient killing rows. The colonists lie scattered in the foreground, among them Crispus Attucks, the first black man killed in the Revolution. If you want to understand Boston, then understand that mural—the Boston massacre and Larry Rivers, the old and the new. Appearances and reality are the key. Dame Boston is a dowager lady who can put on *her* grandmother's pearls and dance all night. Just outside the doors of the bank, tourists walk on the spot where the massacre happened, just below the balconies of the old State House, where the Declaration of Independence was first read to the people. Rising high above the old State House is One Boston Place, a skyscraper that houses the managers of billions of dollars of financial assets from around the world. Its bulk and mirrored surface form a striking backdrop for the small brick building that sits beneath the towers looking just as solid as its newer brethren, although it is the oldest remaining public building in America.

Boston is an intensely personal city. The population in this 355th year since Boston's birth is almost 650,000. With her suburbs, which contain approximately three million people, this whole encompassing metropolitan area is the sixth largest in the nation. There are twenty-one distinct neighborhood districts in the city, many of them neighborhoods where generations of the same family have grown up in turn and remained.

The city had its beginnings in 1630, and was called by the courts 'Boston', after the town in Lincolnshire, England from which the original puritan leaders had come to the New World. In spite of the rigorous puritan rule in Boston's early years, because of its fine harbor the city became the leader in commercial activity. Indeed trade, commerce, and wealth became so important that when English tax restrictions began to prove onerous, the colony rose up in arms. Local agitation grew into revolution in 1775 when the minute men at Lexington, in the words of Emerson's 'Concord Hymn', 'fired the shot heard round the world.' As much as the 'embattled farmers' it was the drawing rooms and counting houses of Boston that were truly responsible for the freedom of the colonies and the birth of the United States of America.

Part of the city's history is the rich legacy of intellectual and scholastic life. Boston is the center of student life in the country. Over one hundred thousand students live in the city, or one out of every six inhabitants. They crowd into apartments in the Allston-Brighton sections, Beacon Hill, the Back Bay, and attend the great nearby universities and colleges, including Harvard, MIT, Boston University, Boston College, Babson, Wellesley, and Tufts. When they matriculate, many stay to enrich this liveable city and add to its diversity and its neighborhoods, melting together into the ethnic areas of Irish, Jewish, Anglo-Saxon, Chinese, Italian, and Hispanic. The newcomers put down their roots, nestle into the history and delve into a literary tradition springing from Emerson, Thoreau, Longfellow, Oliver Wendell Holmes, Francis Parkman, and Louisa May Alcott. Mark Twain, speaking there one hundred years ago, said 'Tomorrow night I appear for the first time before a Boston audience...four thousand critics.' There is an intellectual curiosity that goes with being a center of learning. The arts thrive in a city that has major museums, diverse and historic architecture, from Charles Bulfinch's gilt-domed State House to H.H. Richardson's Trinity Church, to I.M. Pei's controversial Hancock Tower. The Boston Symphony is one of the finest orchestras in the world. On any one evening a Bostonian has literally dozens of choices in theatre, dance, or music. Even in the world of the arts there is again this theme of contrasts, appearances and reality. Boston loves her sports—football, basketball, hockey, the Boston Marathon, rowing on the Charles River. But probably baseball is dearest to the heart of the citizen, baseball at Fenway Park with the Red Sox. A hero like Ted Williams is one of Boston's idols, and arguably the best hitter in the history of the sport. 'The splendid sprinter (Williams) hit a home run his last time at bat. The papers said that the other players and even the umpires in the field begged him to come out and acknowledge us in some way, but he never had and did not now. Gods do not answer letters.' Poetry to praise a Boston legend. Poetry from a Boston literary hero, John Updike writing for the *New Yorker*.

Politics as practiced in Boston has always been a spectator sport. Modern Boston politics really began with 'Honey Fitz' Fitzgerald, grandfather of President John F. Kennedy. The Irish have always considered themselves the 'oppressed majority' in the city and have ruled with flamboyance, strength, and style since World War I. James Michael Curley, long-time mayor, won an election while serving a jail term. He has been captured forever in Edwin O'Connor's classic novel *The Last Hurrah*, which personified Boston's colorful political traditions. O'Connor himself lived in the shadow of the State House on Beacon Hill and his literary descendants, the novelists who meet as neighbors in the city, now include James Carroll, Dan Wakefield, Robin Cook, and mystery writer Robert Parker.

Boston is in many ways more like a small town than a city, so personal. Former Mayor Kevin White gave a speech in the Back Bay section at the Institute of Contemporary Art, in which he made reference to U.S. presidential administrations under James Polk and James Buchanan in the mid-1800s that had been 'less than stellar'. After the speech, White was moving through the crowd. A man approached him and said, 'You just lost *my* vote.'

'Lost your vote?' the Mayor questioned. 'I'd like to know why?'

'Because,' the man said seriously, 'you insulted President Polk. James Polk was my *great*-grandfather.' Only in Boston are you likely to hear a story like that, a story where the past is taken so seriously, a past that affects the present. The diversity of the city's politics is a drum-roll of illustrious names; John McCormack and Thomas P. 'Tip' O'Neil, Elliot Richardson, Leverett Saltonstall, John Volpe, Henry Cabot Lodge, John F. Kennedy, Bobby Kennedy, Ted Kennedy....

The face of Boston has changed enormously over the years but again the contrast is apparent. New development has made Boston, in the view of major banks, the hottest city to which to loan money in America. Major projects pepper the town with activity, from the Prudential Center to the Hancock Tower to I.M. Pei's Christian Science Center, to the three-hundred-million-dollar Copley Place on one of the most handsome waterfronts in the world. The heart of the city is probably its public living-room, Quincy Market Place and Faneuil Hall. Faneuil Hall, called the 'cradle of the American revolution' because of its ancient role as a meeting house, has been restored as a landmark, with a quarter of a million square feet of commercial space surrounding it on almost seven acres. A granite Greek revival shopping center and parallel North and South Markets attract more than a million visitors a month, 'more than Disney World', it is widely trumpeted. Along with physical development, the business climate of Boston has boomed in recent years, with unemployment in Massachusetts the lowest of all the major industrial states. High technology, along with financial services and construction, have been largely responsible for this growth. Companies like Digital Equipment, Wang Labs, Data General, contribute to Boston's reputation as a leader in technology, builders of over 70 percent of all mini-computers made in the United States. Major corporations, like Gillette, Sheraton, Stride Rite, General Cinema, Raytehon and Honeywell, give back money and jobs to the community. And Boston always has been, from the days of the whaling ships and the three-cornered trade, a leader in the industry of managing and guarding people's money; the home of the mutual fund, trustee to billions of dollars from all over the world.

Ever present in history, song, and story is the sea. Colonists arrived by boat. They sent back their own ships laden with New World goods and the ideas of freedom that represented the true American revolution. Along Commonwealth Avenue, running the length of the Back Bay section, there is a mall of grass, trees, and statues—many of them honoring the role of the sea in Boston's history. One of the statues is that of Leif Erikson, the Viking explorer. Another is of Boston's most important historian of the oceans, Admiral Samuel Eliot Morison, who wrote of the early Boston Yankees 'a tough but nervous, tenacious yet restless race, materially ambitious, they are prone to introspection, and subject to waves of religious emotion...a race whose typical member is eternally torn between a passion for righteousness and a desire to get on in the world.' Morison's statue shows him seated on a rock, as if staring out to sea. But his gaze also would take in the skyscrapers of the city, would take in the seats of power in commerce and banking, and government and high technology. His gaze would take in all the cultural institutions. It is the weather-beaten look of the sailor, with the understanding of the historian, full of memories of the past, full of hope for the future of Boston.

JOHN D. SPOONER

1 The site of the Boston Massacre is marked by this circle of cobblestones in front of the Old State House. On 5 March 1770, British soldiers killed former slave Crispus Attucks and four others.

2 A commuter boat ferries passengers between Logan Airport and downtown Boston.

3 *(right)* Crewing exercises on the Charles River.

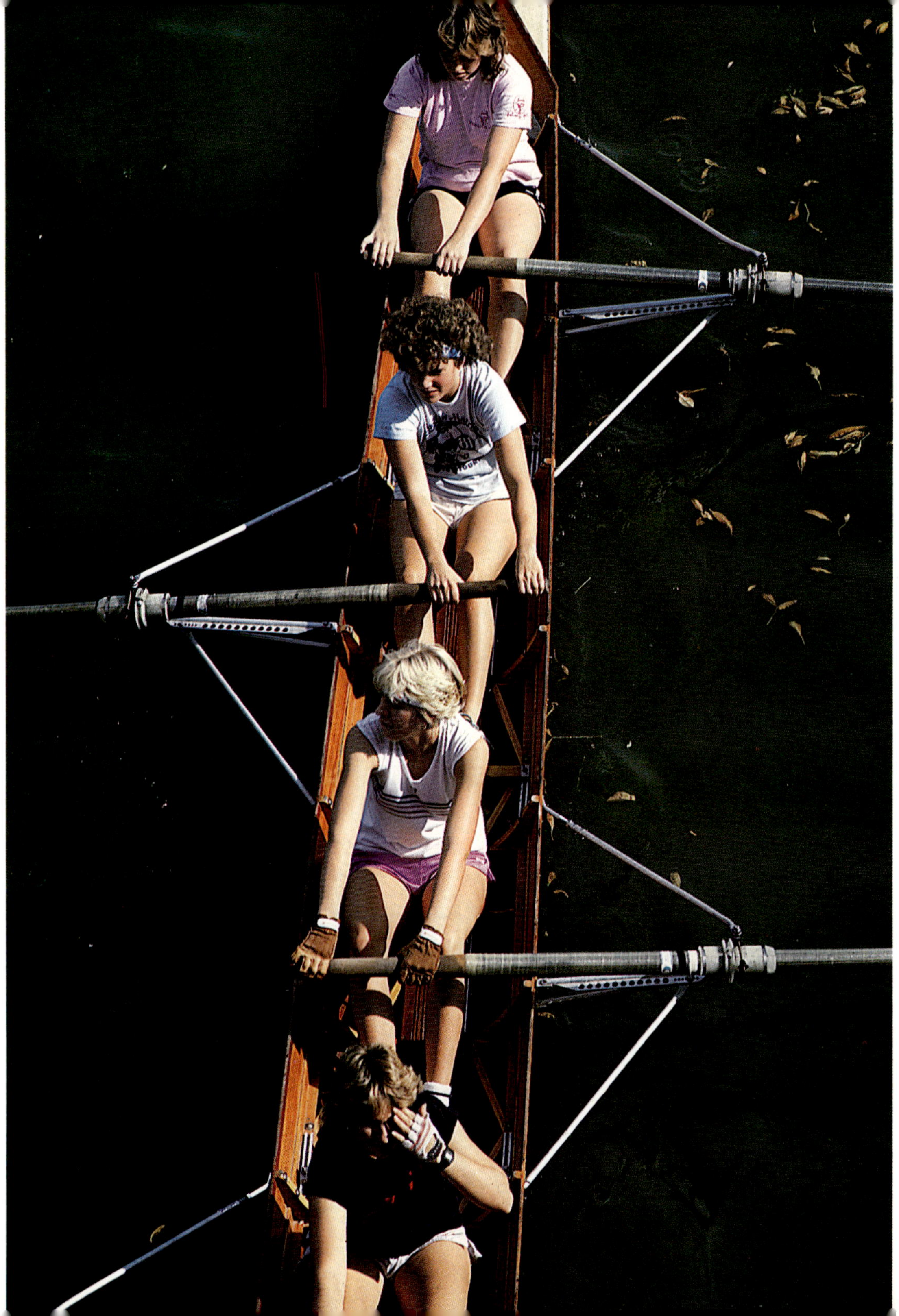

4 The Paul Revere House, built in 1680, was occupied by Revere a century later. It was the first house to be preserved and restored in the United States.

5 Haymarket.

6 This sundial located on the Old State House was recreated from Paul Revere's engraving of the Boston Massacre.

7 The Hall of Flags at the State House contains over 300 flags. The tradition of 'returning the colors' started in 1865 after the Civil War. Flags have been returned after duty in every war since. The stained-glass skylight contains the seal of the original thirteen colonies with Massachusetts in the center.

8 The House of Representatives is viewed from the public galleries. The walls are lined with the Albert Herta murals *Milestones on the road to freedom*. Here the 160-member legislative body conducts its business and votes electronically. Above hangs the Sacred Cod.

9 *(right)* The Park Street Church.

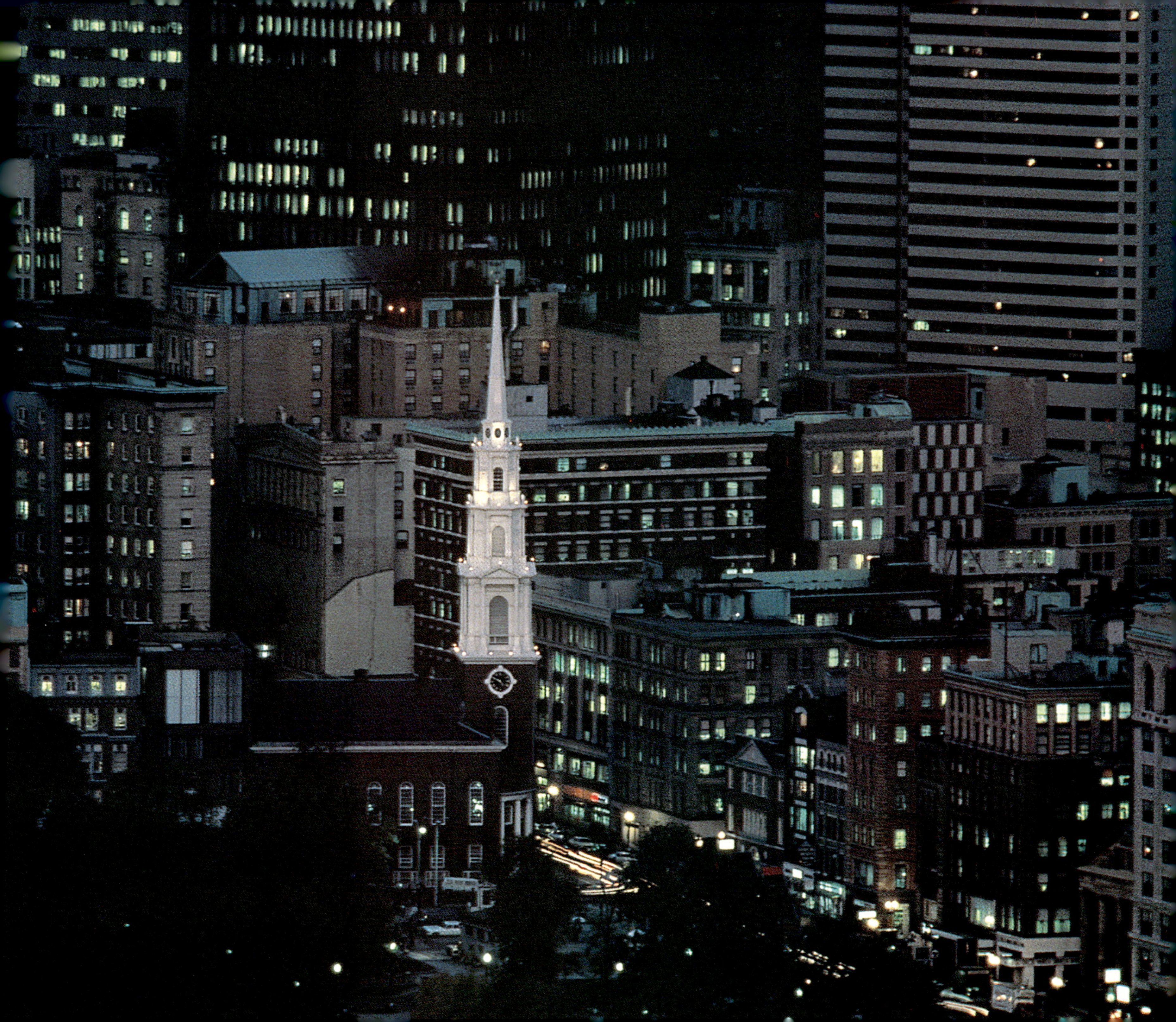

10 A copperplate engraving by Paul Revere depicts the occupation of Boston by British troops in 1768.

11 *(right)* A fishing schooner rests quietly in Boston Harbor.

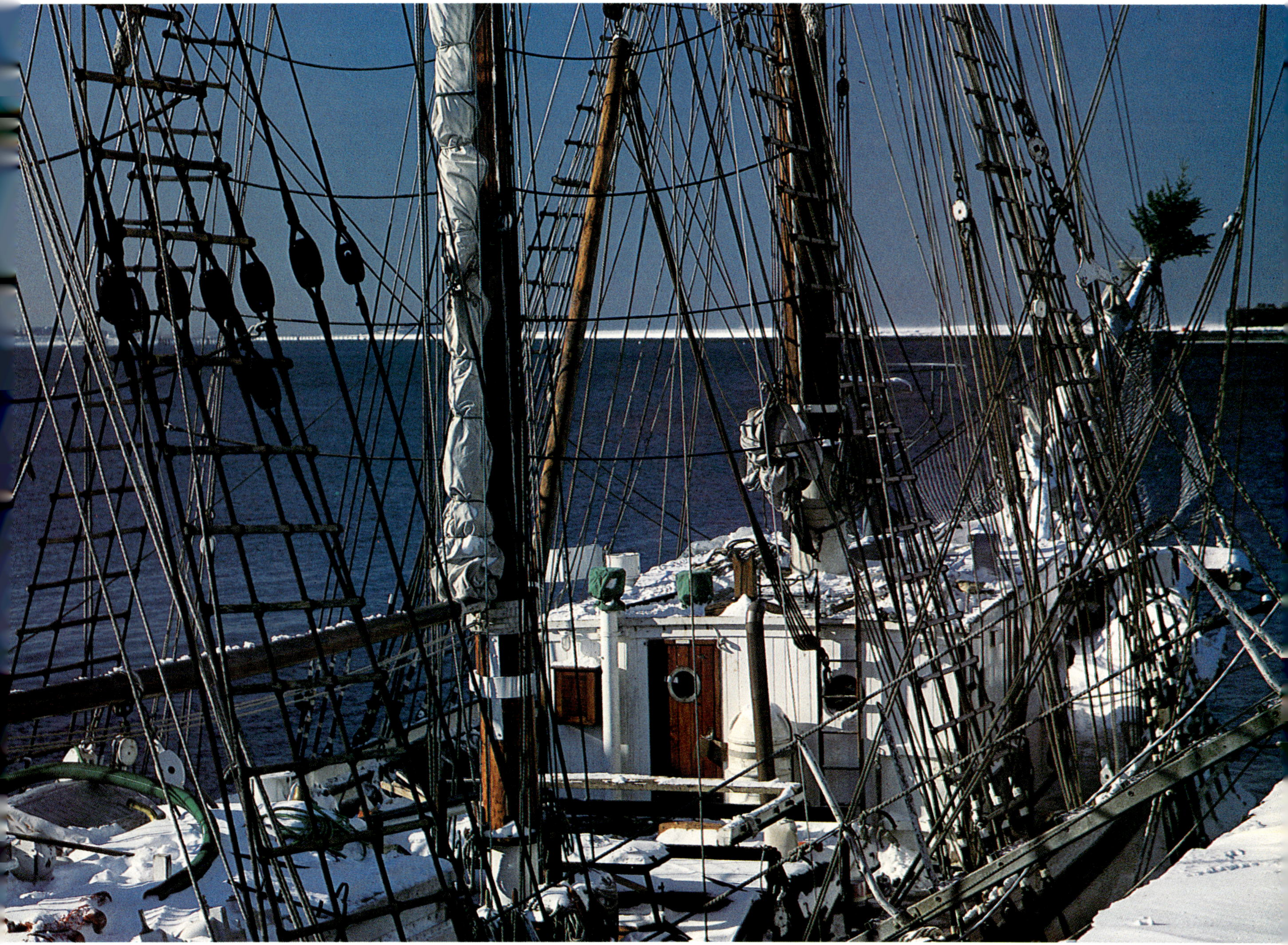

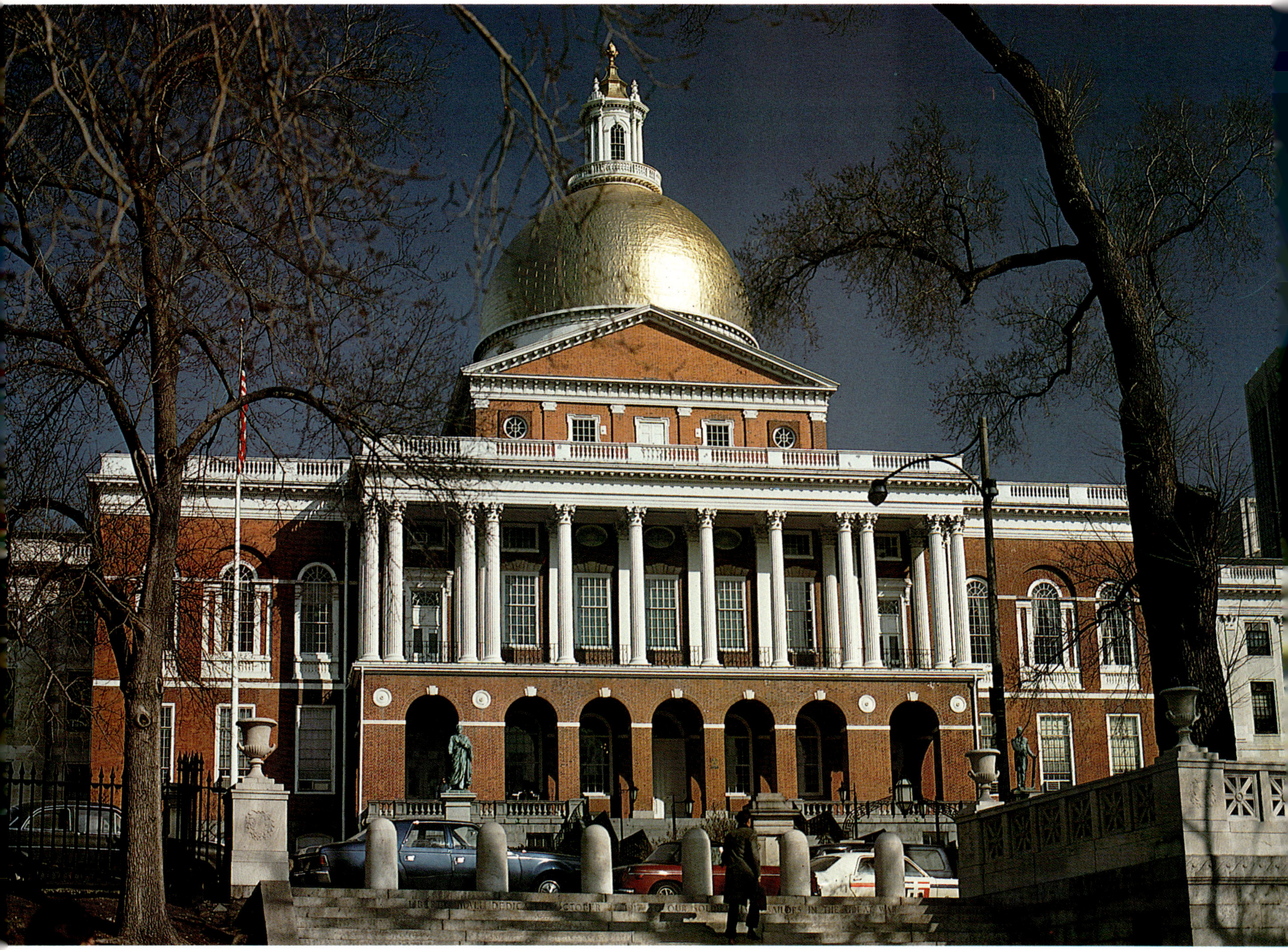

12 *(left)* The gold dome of the State House gleams in the afternoon sun. Built on land belonging to the John Hancock family, it is the oldest structure on Beacon Hill. The front and dome were designed by Charles Bulfinch.

13 *Ben Franklin* is Boston's first portrait sculpture (1856). The sculptor, Richard S. Greenough, gave each profile a different expression.

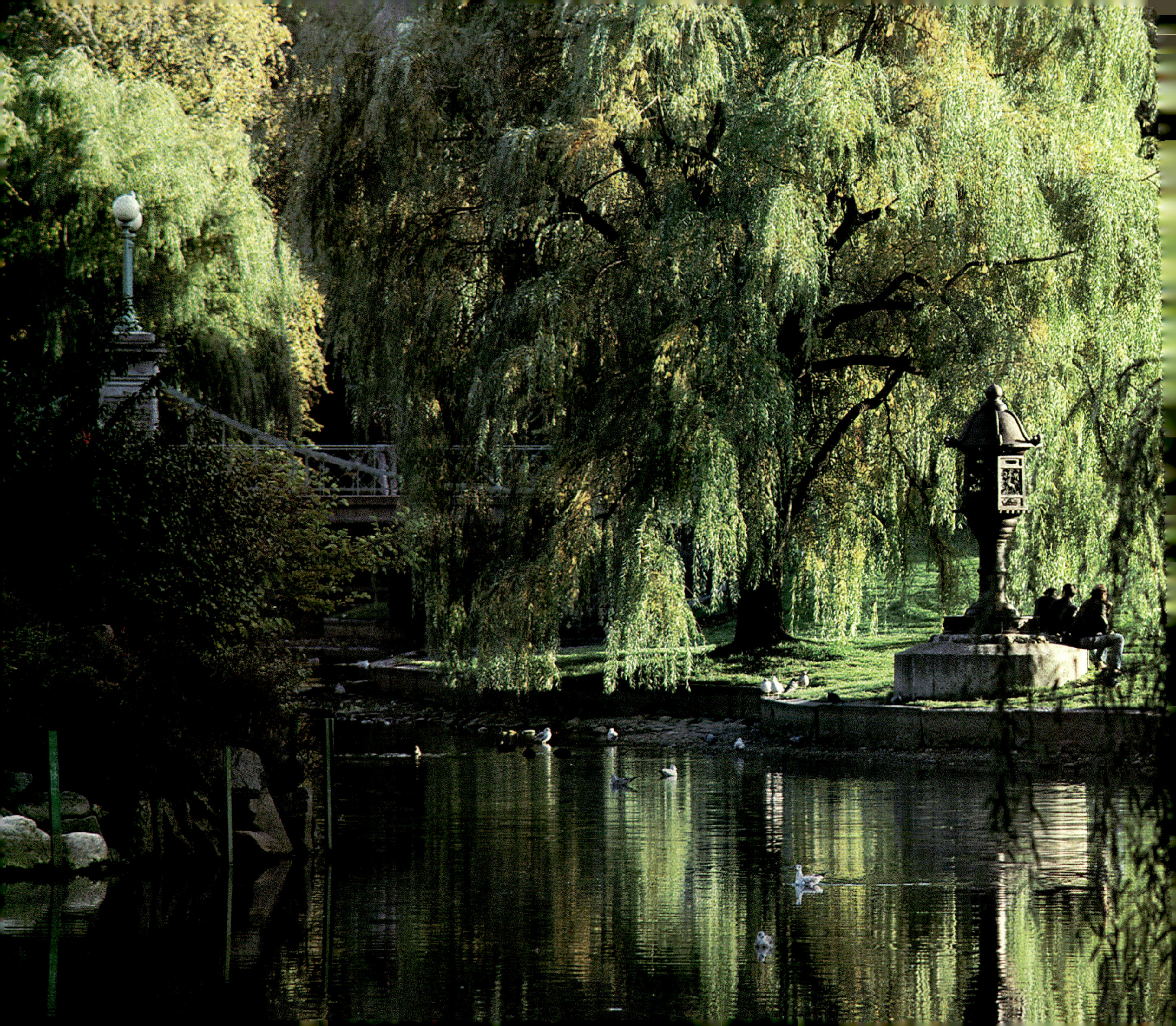

14 *(left)* The man-made pond at Boston Public Gardens.

15 The Public Garden.

16 Fishermen repairing their nets.

17 Lobster traps on Pier One.

18 Haymarket tomatoes.

19 The steeple of the Old West Church was torn down by the British in 1776 to prevent it from being used as a signal tower as the Old North Church was.

20 Offshore lobster boat. Lobsters were once so abundant that they were gathered from the beaches of New England. It is said that the Pilgrims considered them to be peasant food.

21 Boston's Haymarket is located between fashionable Faneuil Hall and the Italian North End. Vendors compete to sell fresh produce from their carts.

22 Morning light on Boston Harbor.

23 *(right)* Fishing boats steam away from the dock.

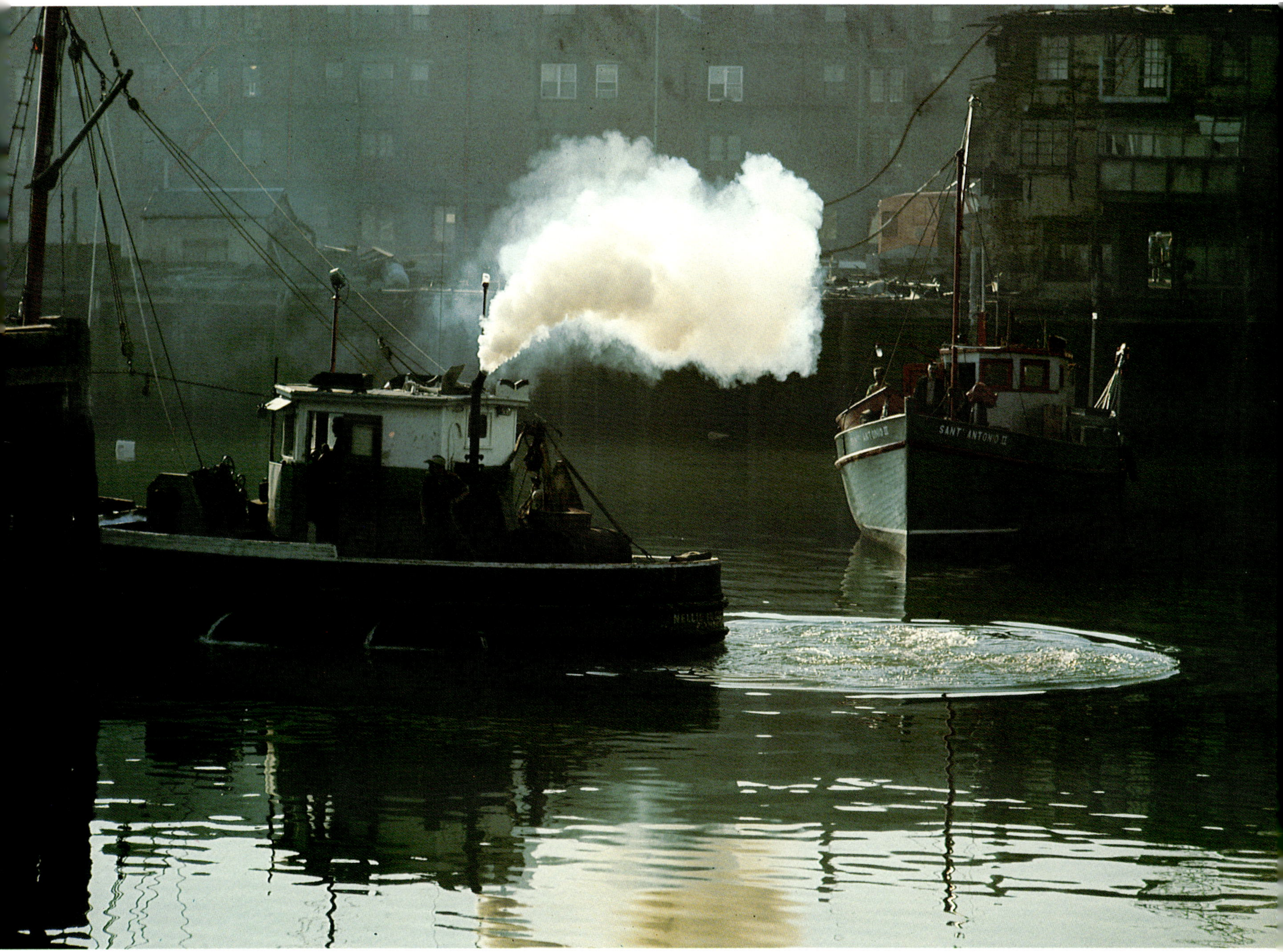
SANT' ANTONIO II

24 The Boston Public Library or the B.P.L. is the oldest free library in the world. It was built in 1888–1895 by McKim, Mead & White.

25 Faneuil Hall was built for the town of Boston in 1742 by Peter Faneuil, a wealthy French Huguenot merchant. The market and meeting place has also been called 'The Cradle Of Liberty' because it was here that the American Revolutionary spirit was said to have been born.

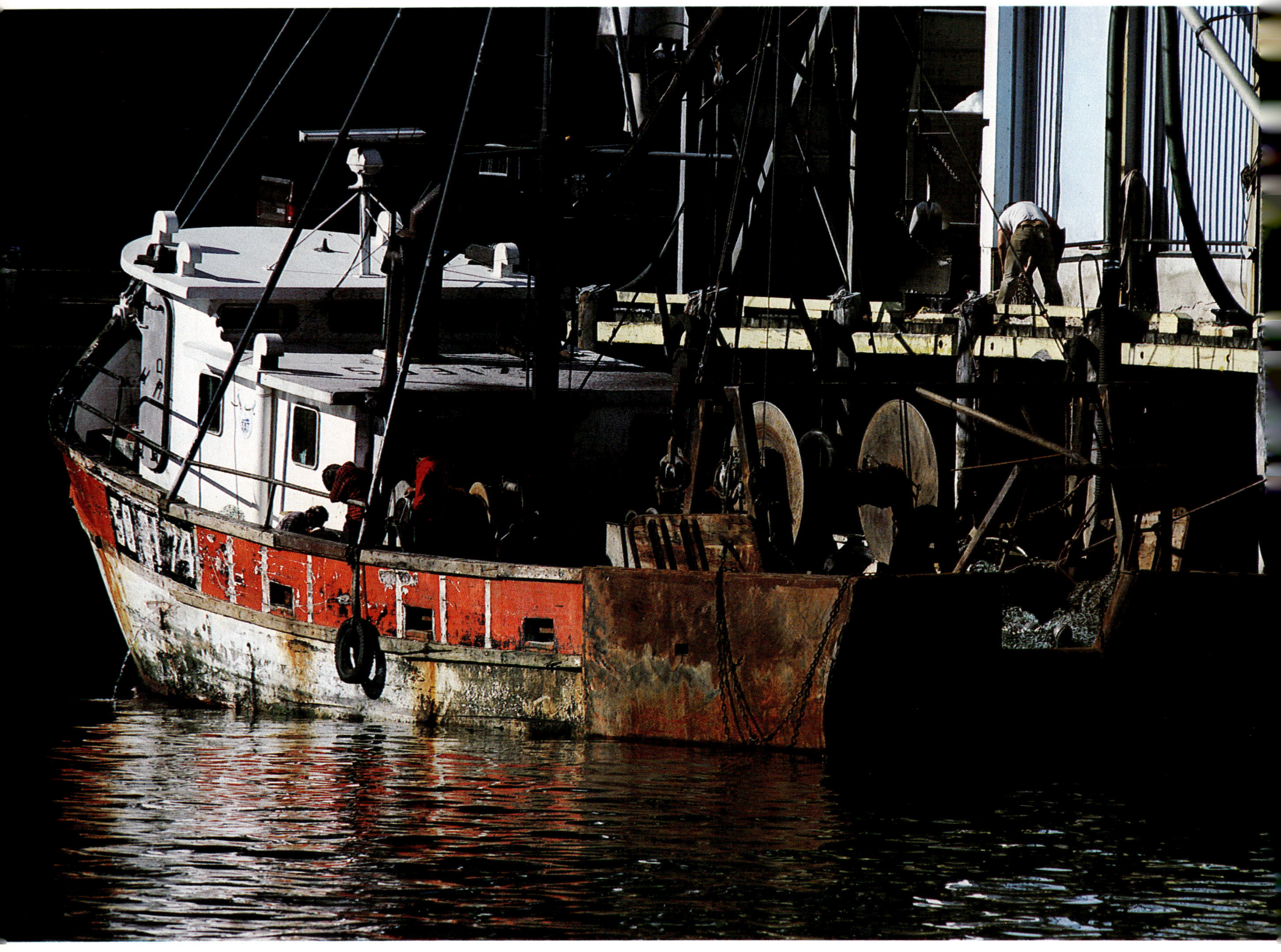

26 *(left)* Fishing boat at Pier Six.

27 Converted warehouses on Commercial and Lewis wharf are now a chic environment in which to live or work on Boston's waterfront.

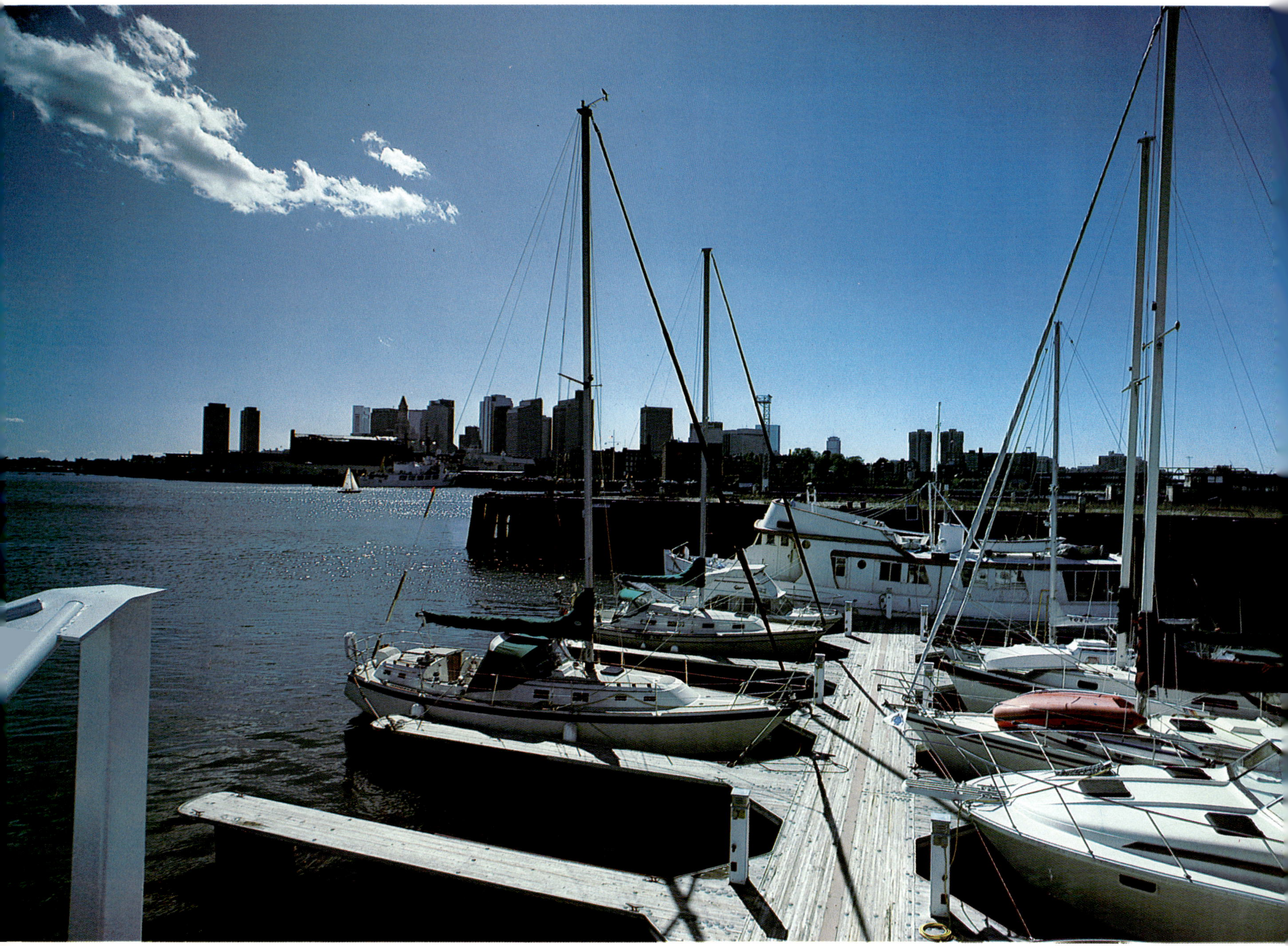

28 *(left)* Nearby, Charlestown offers a peaceful view of the city from a newly constructed Marina.

29 The crew prepares for another day of lobstering.

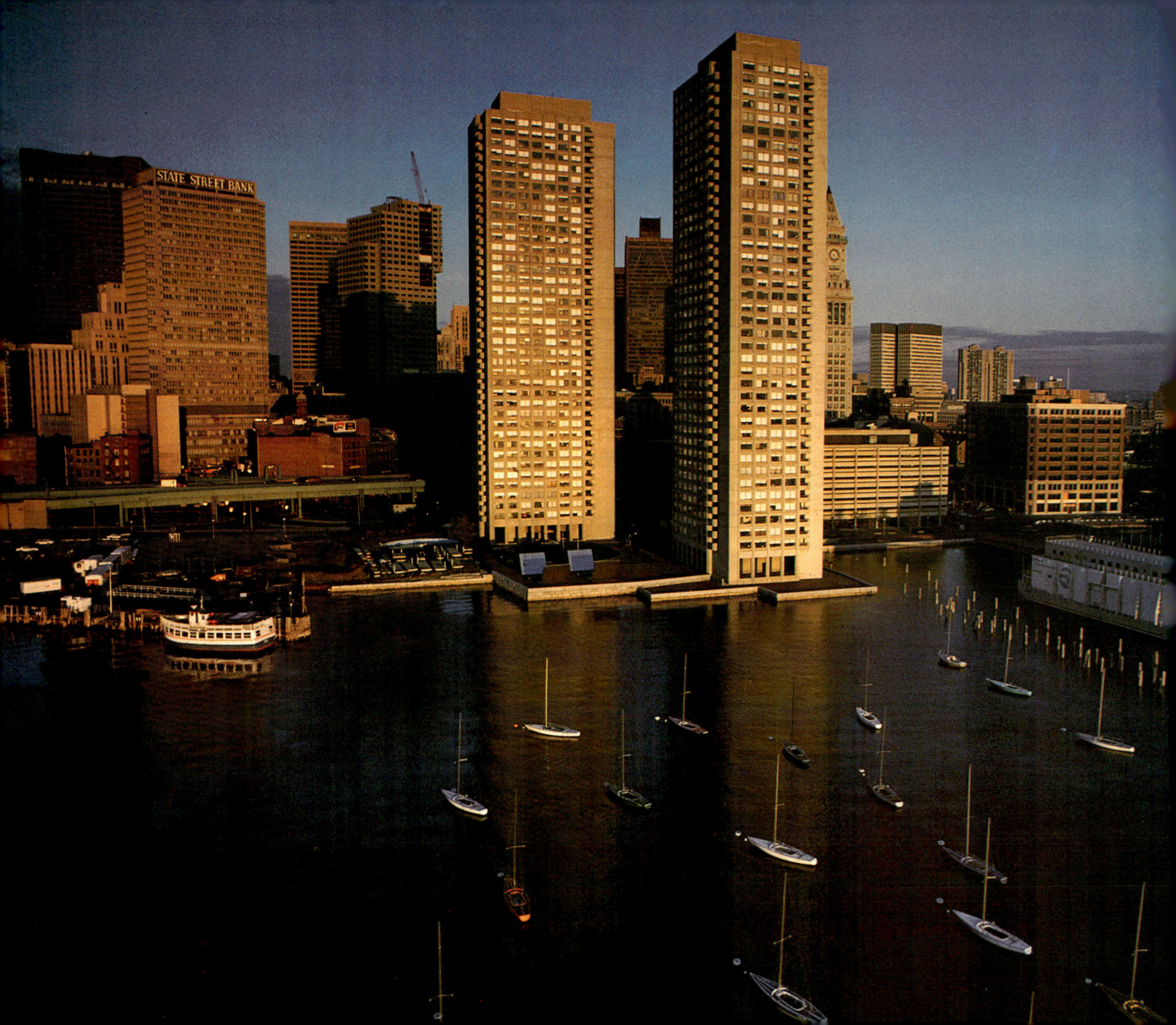
STATE STREET BANK

30 *(left)* Harbor Towers twin buildings dominate the harbor skyline at sunrise.

31 Each year the Feast Of Saint Anthony is celebrated in Boston's North End. It begins with a procession and ends with feasting in the streets.

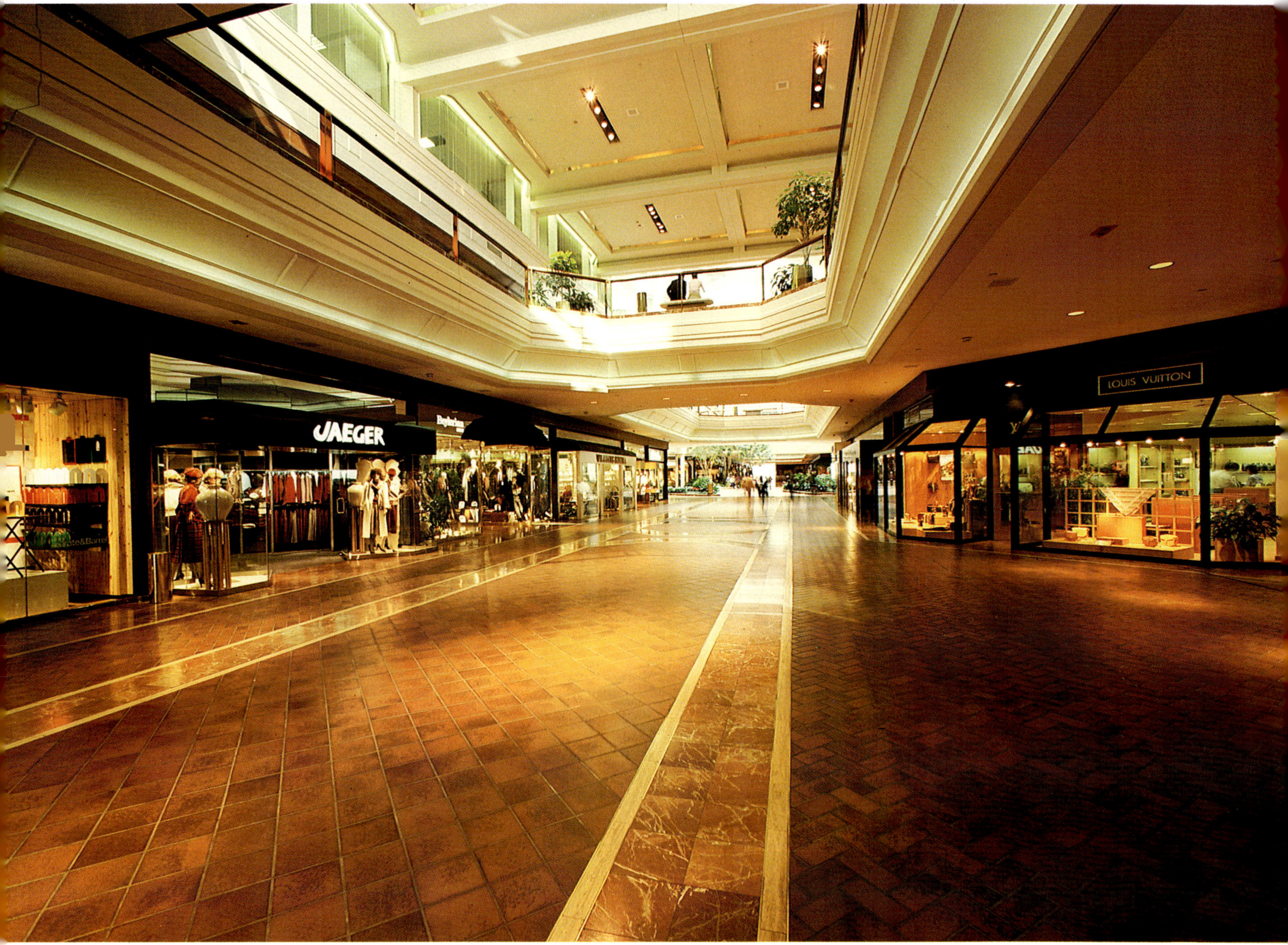
JAEGER
LOUIS VUITTON

32 *(left)* Copley Place, designed by the Architects Collaborative, is a mixed-use complex. The modern development is one of the largest of its kind in the United States.

33 The Massport Moran Terminal which opened in 1972 is the largest container terminal in New England. It handles some 45,000 containers per year.

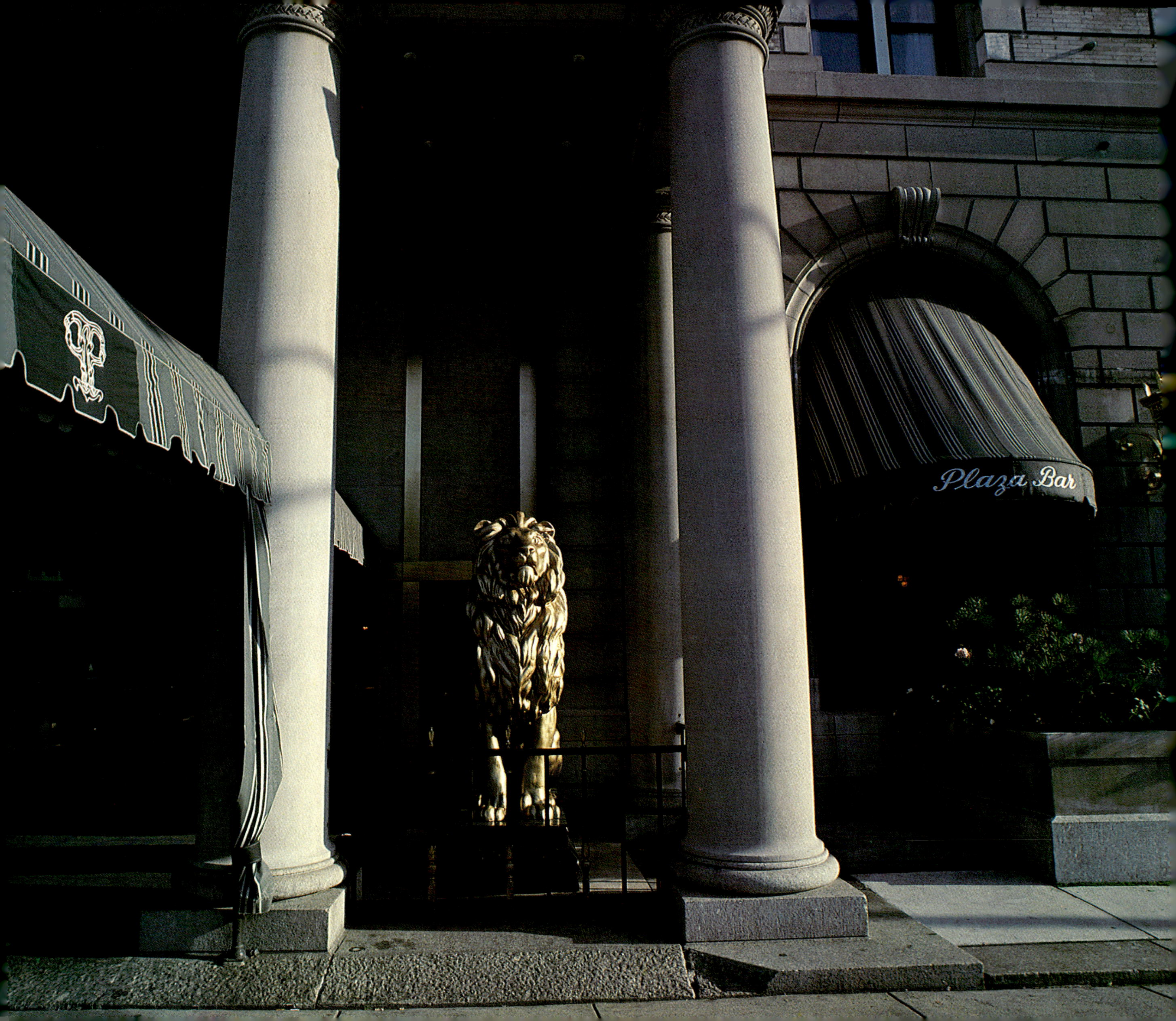
Plaza Bar

34 *(left)* Built on the site of the original Museum of Fine Arts, The Copley Plaza Hotel is known locally as the grande dame of the city. It was built in 1912 by Clarence H. Blackall and Henry Hardenburg.

35 Public Gardens.

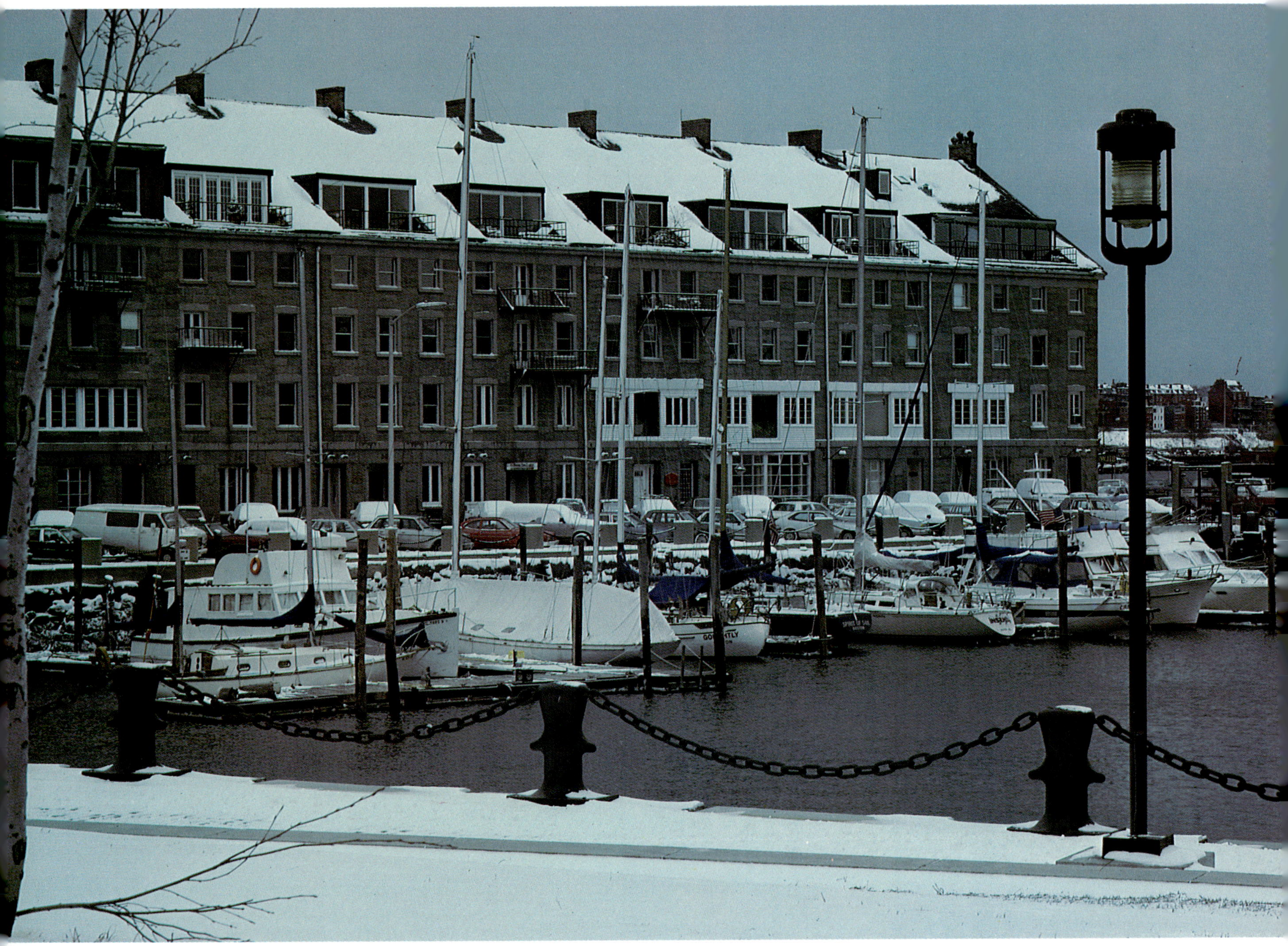

36 *(left)* Commercial Wharf awakes to a dusting of snow.

37 In spring, the magnolia trees all but obscure the famous architecture of Commonwealth Avenue.

38 A towboat under the Tobin Bridge on its way to Moran Terminal.

39 *(right)* The U.S.S. *Constitution*, known as 'Old Ironsides', is the world's oldest warship still under commission. Every Fourth of July she has a ceremonious turnaround so that her hull will weather evenly.

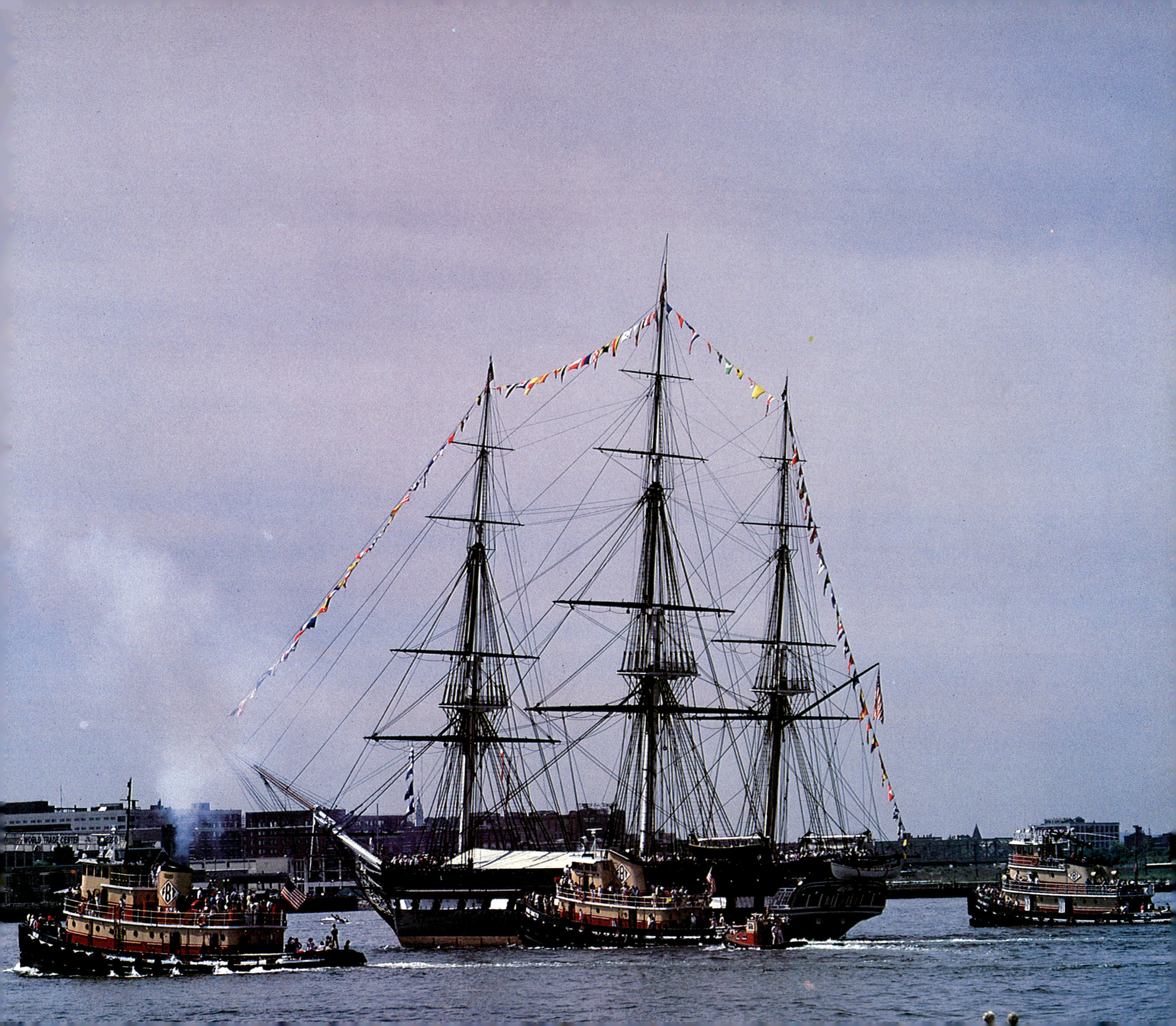
WORLD TRADE CENTER

40 The New England Aquarium, opened in 1969. A giant 187,000-gallon ocean tank allows visitors a three-story view of the deep and its residents. Friendly seals give free performances in an outside pen by the entrance.

41 The magnificent Custom House Tower seen from the west corner of New City Hall. Built in 1847, it was originally located on the water's edge before landfill increased its distance from the harbor.

42 Ferry-boat in Boston Harbor.

43 At the Commonwealth Avenue entrance to the Public Garden stands a forceful tribute to General George Washington. It is Boston's first equestrian statue. The 38-foot bronze monument was created by Thomas Ball in 1869.

44 Modern glass tower at Exchange Place was built 40 stories high by Olympia & York Construction and finished in 1985.

45 *(right)* Lewis Wharf.

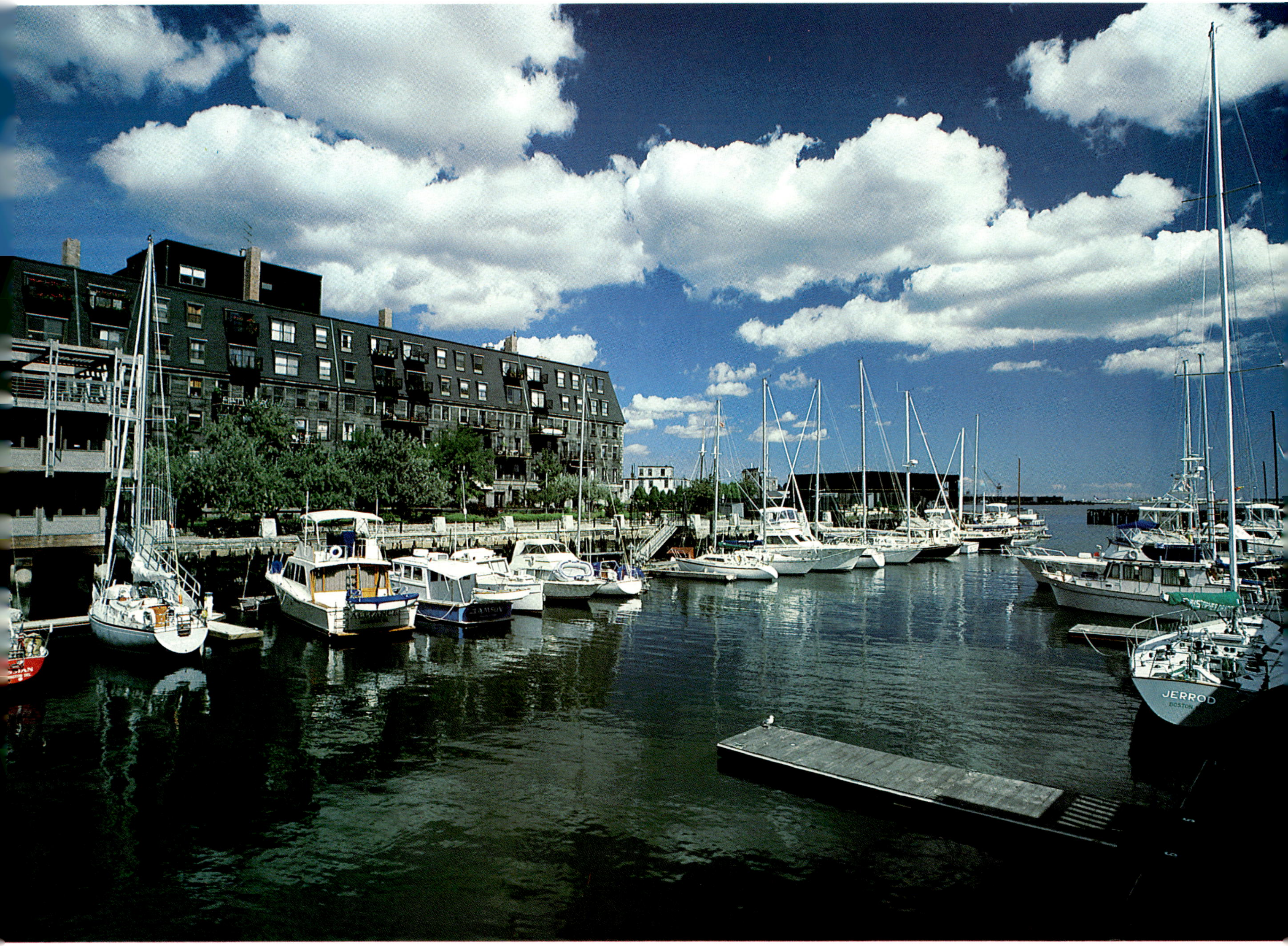
JERROD
BOSTON

46 This Back Bay mansion was formerly owned by railroad tycoon Frederic L. Ames and is known today as the Webster House. The grand staircase is three stories high and topped by a domed ceiling lined with stained glass (John La Farge). It was designed in 1872 by Peabody & Stearns and altered ten years later by John Stargis.

47 39 Beacon Street was the home of Nathan Appleton. His daughter Fanny married Henry Wadsworth Longfellow in this house. The intricately carved marble fireplace is one of two in the country. The other is in the White House. See also plate 76.

48 Built in 1713, the Old State House was considered to be the Hub of Boston Politics. The Boston Massacre occurred on this site in 1770, and the Declaration of Independence was first read to the public from the balcony in 1776.

49 A lion and a unicorn stand on top of the Old State House as symbols of British royalty. They are copies, however, the originals having been burned by angry patriots when the British pulled out.

50 Flag Day is officially observed on Beacon Hill.

51 *(right)* Louisburg Square is the essence of Beacon Hill tradition. Carolling fills the air and windows are candle-lit on Christmas Eve.

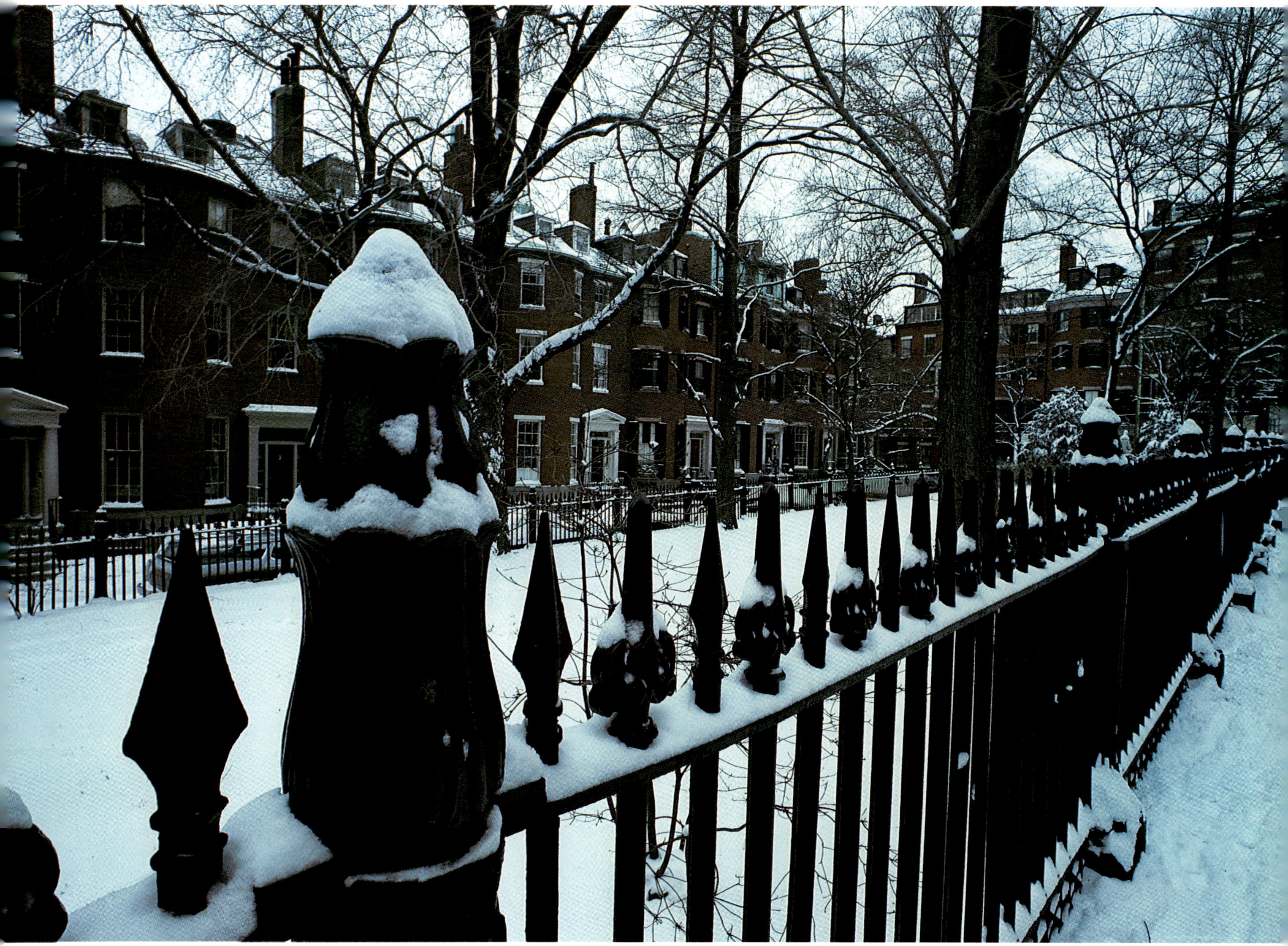

52 The Esplanade bridge on the Charles River is a favorite spot for cyclists, joggers and strollers of all ages.

53 The *Bluenose II* glides out of Boston Harbor on her way home to Nova Scotia.

54 Thousands gather along the river banks for the Boston Pops Annual Fourth of July Celebration followed by fireworks.

55 *(right)* The Boston Pops finish their season with free outdoor summer concerts in the Hatch Memorial Shell on the Charles River Esplanade.

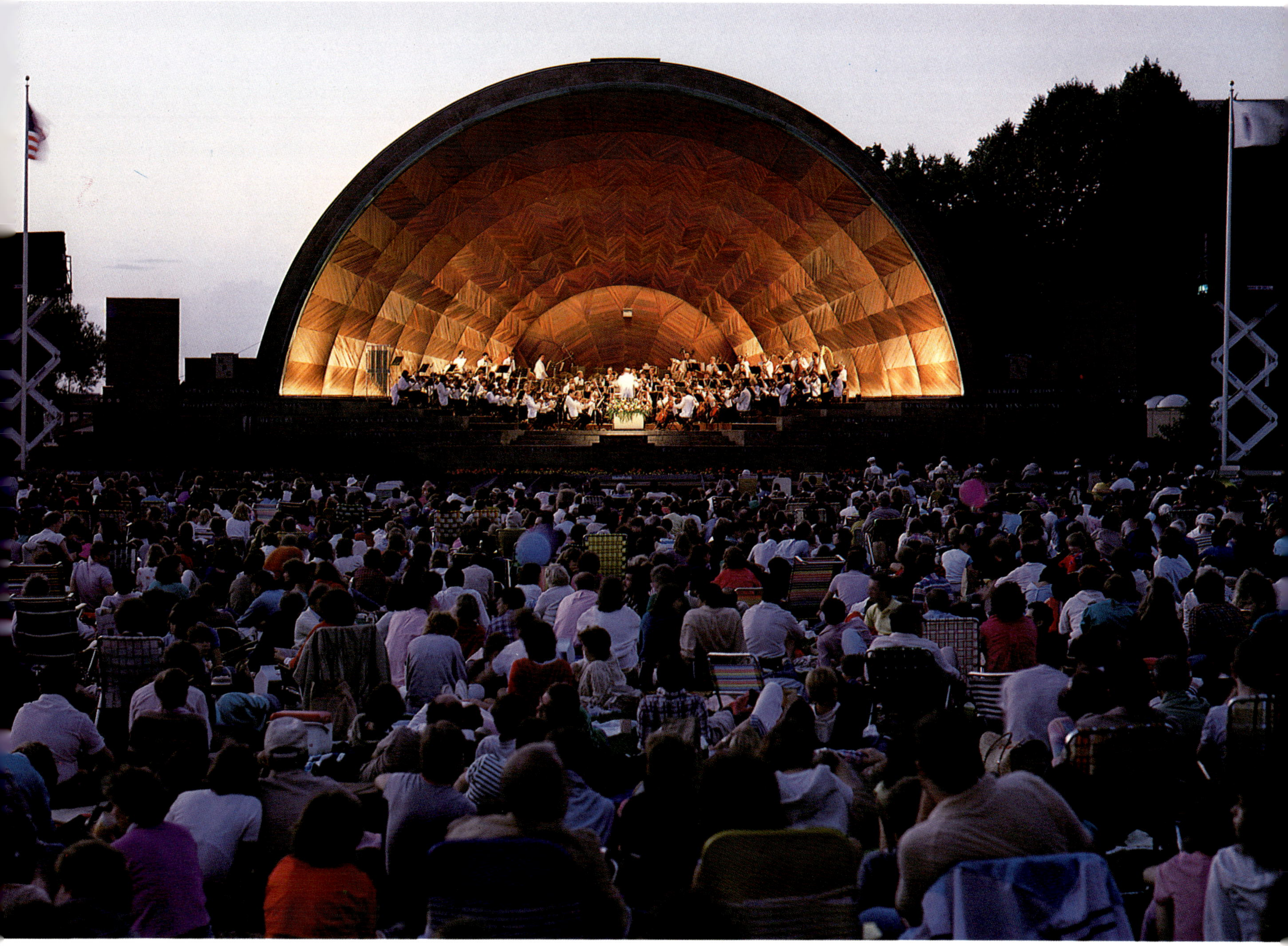

56 Fresh lobster is delivered daily to the many seafood restaurants in the city.

57 *(right)* Fish is the cry at Haymarket. If you're not buying, move along.

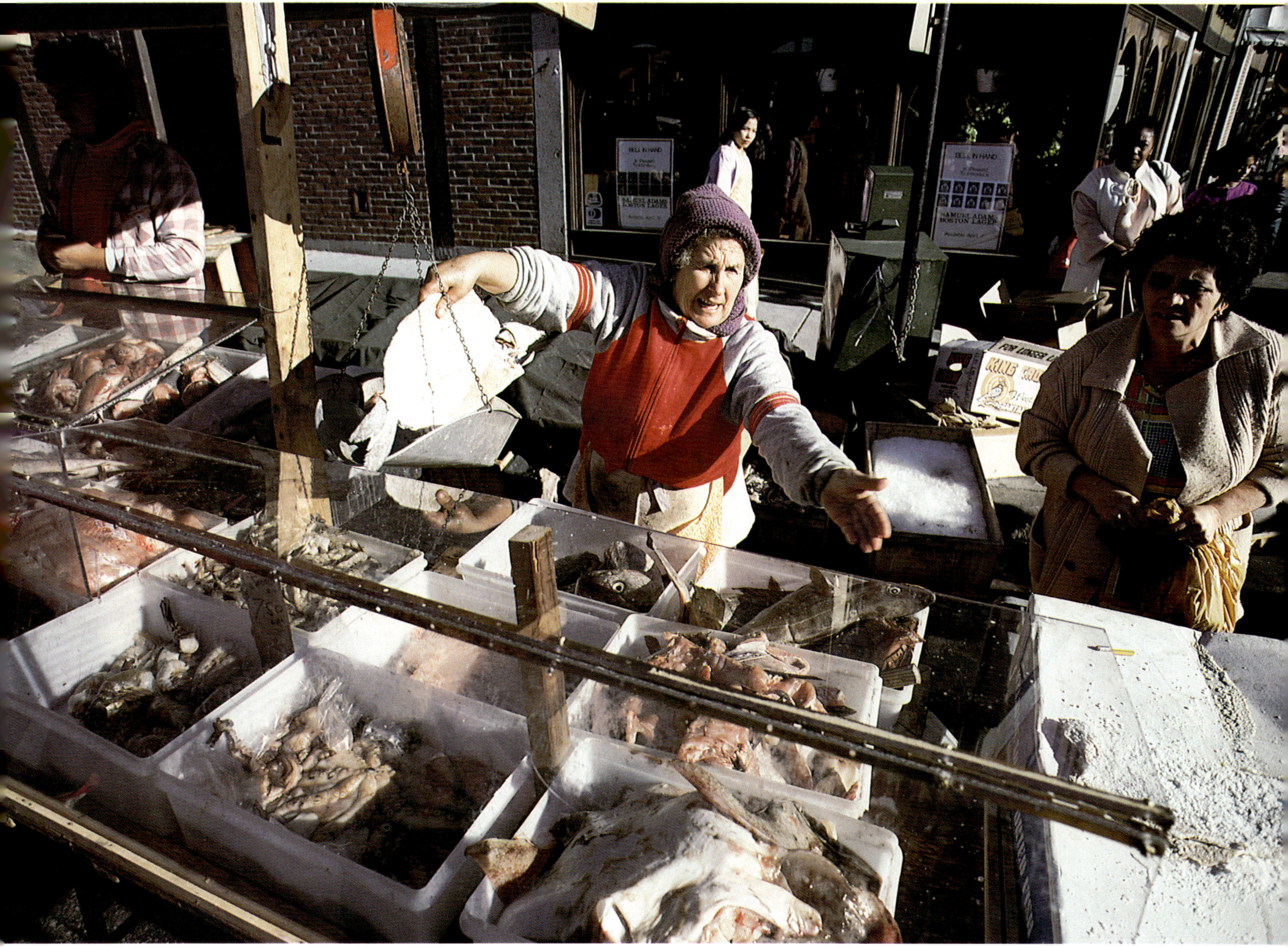
BELL IN HAND
BOSTON LAGER

58 The worldwide headquarters of the Christian Science Church.

59 *(right)* Isabella Stewart Gardner designed this museum which bears her name. The Venetian-style palace serves as a setting for a distinguished art collection, flower shows and weekly concerts. Mrs. Gardner established an endowment 'for the education and enjoyment of the public forever.'

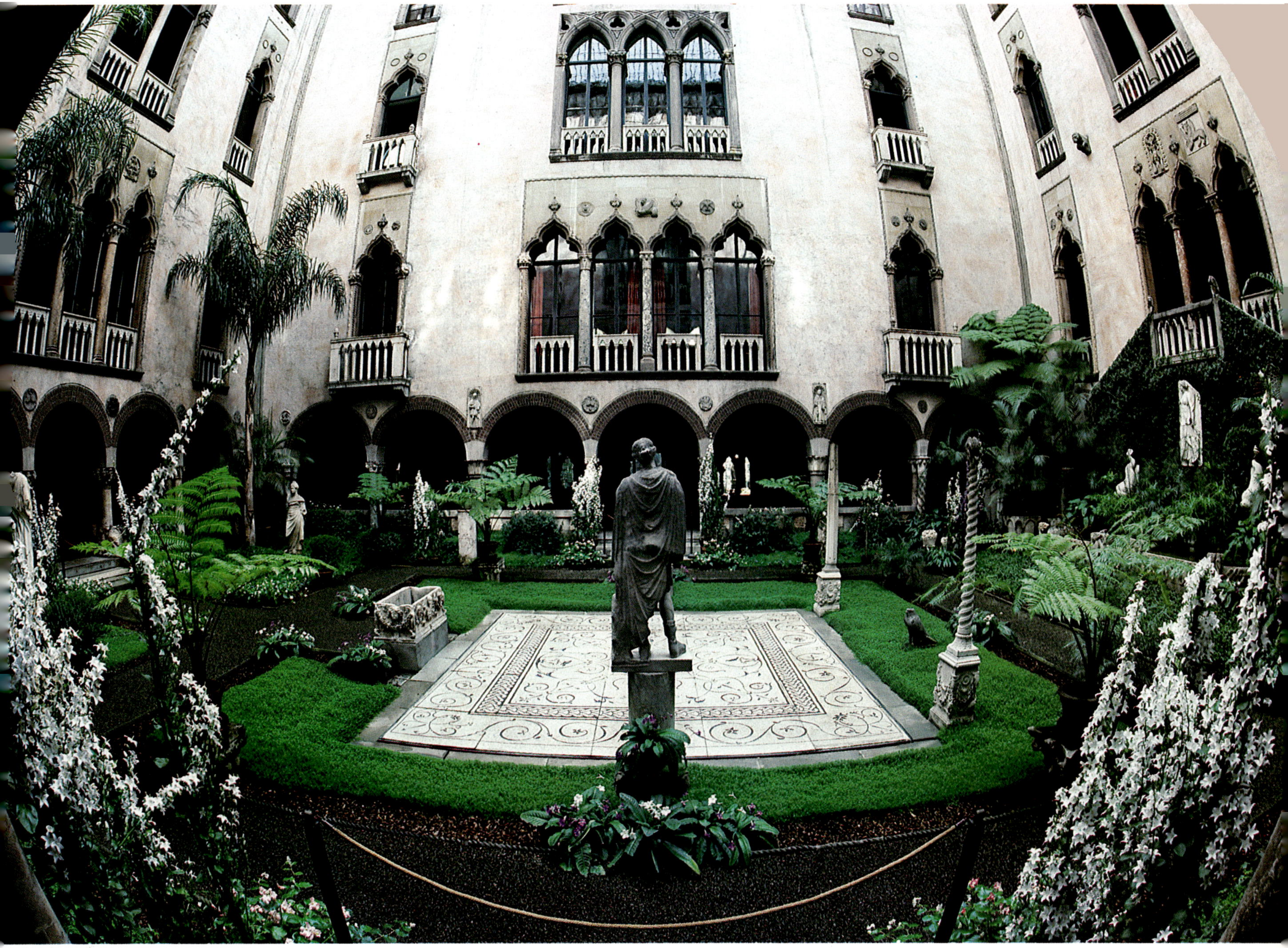

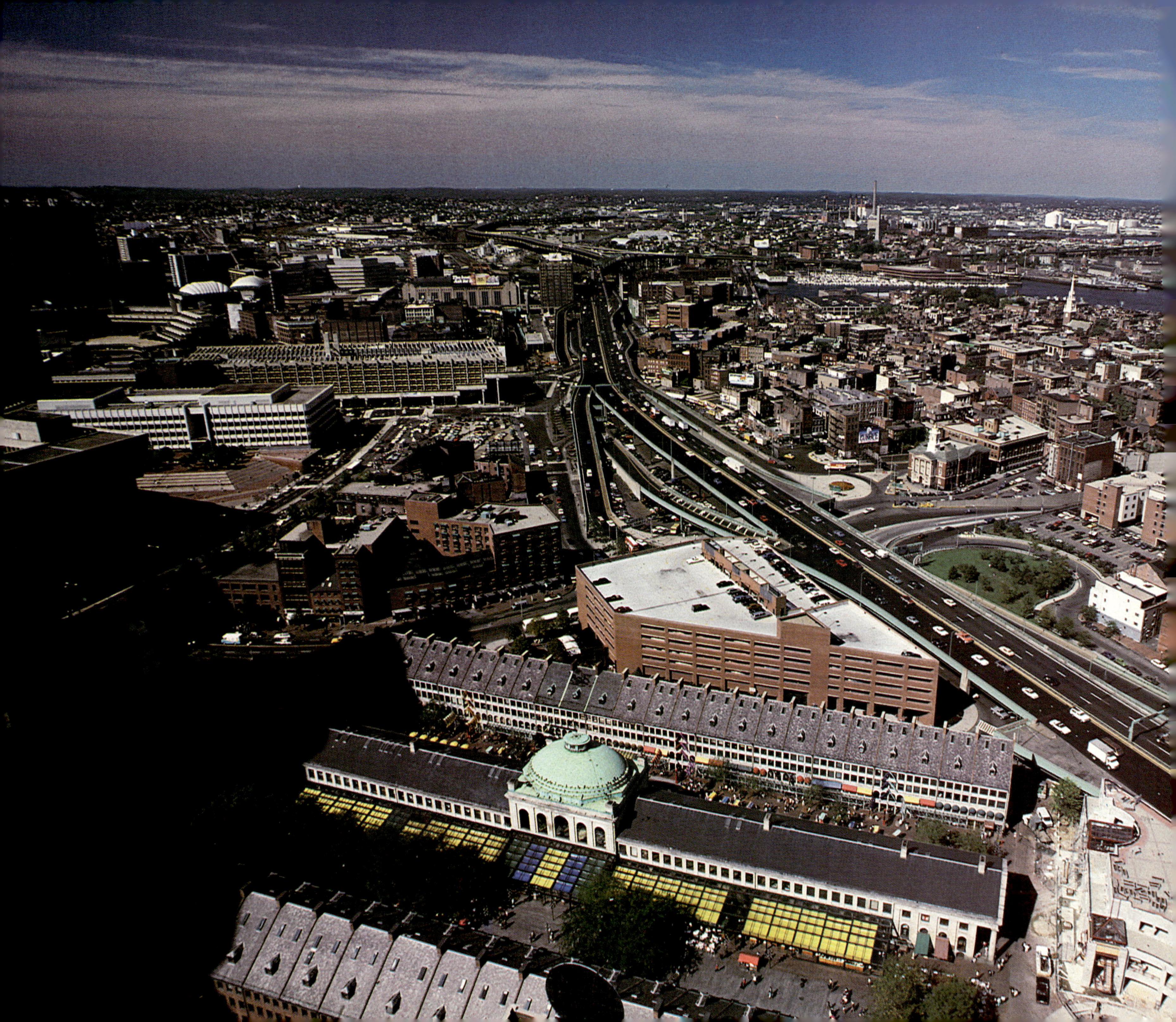

60 *(left)* Overview of Quincy Market Place and Faneuil Hall from the Customs House.

61 The famous Boston Marathon begins in Hopkington some 26 miles away. The race attracts eight to nine thousand official runners and a thousand unofficial ones every Patriots' Day. The custom began in 1897.

62 Trinity Church provides a historic foreground for the modern John Hancock tower.

63 *(right)* The Coast Guard cutter *Hamilton* was named after Alexander Hamilton who was Secretary of the Treasury at the inception of the 'Revenue Marine' in 1790.

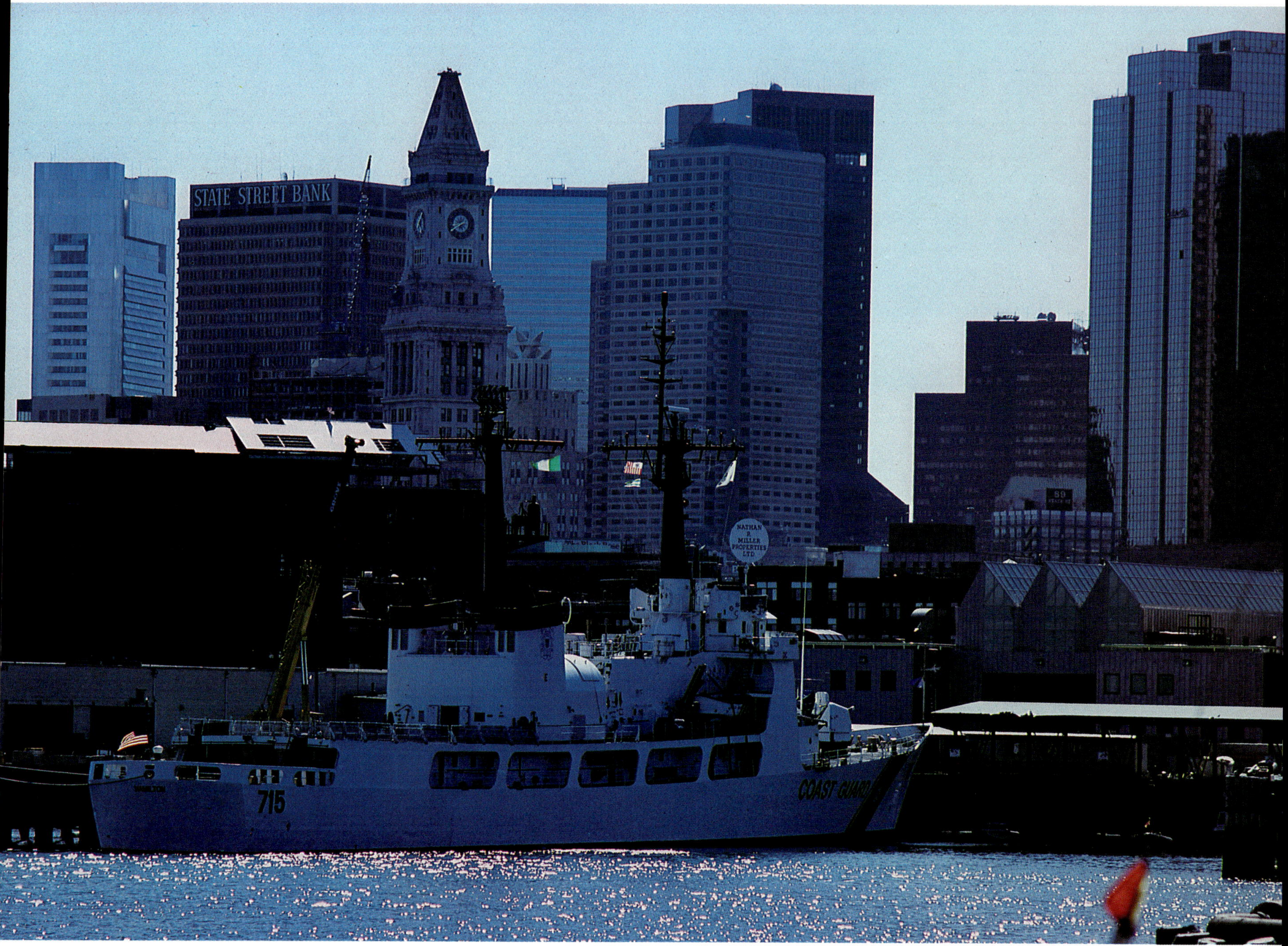
STATE STREET BANK
715
COAST GUARD

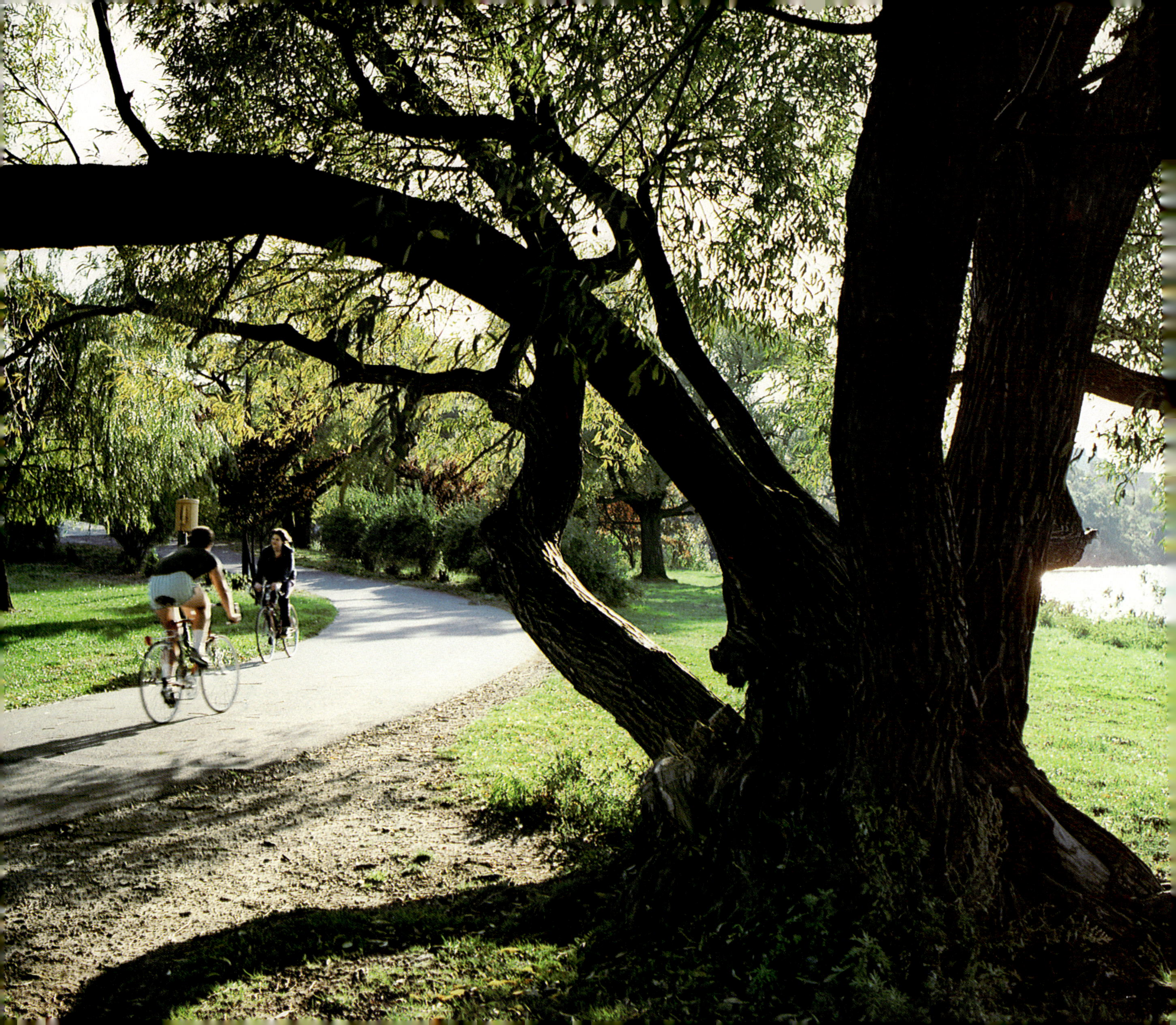

64 *(left)* The Charles River Esplanade.

65 In the 1850's, clipper ships made Lewis Wharf their home during the California Gold Rush. In the 1960's the old warehouses were converted into condominiums.

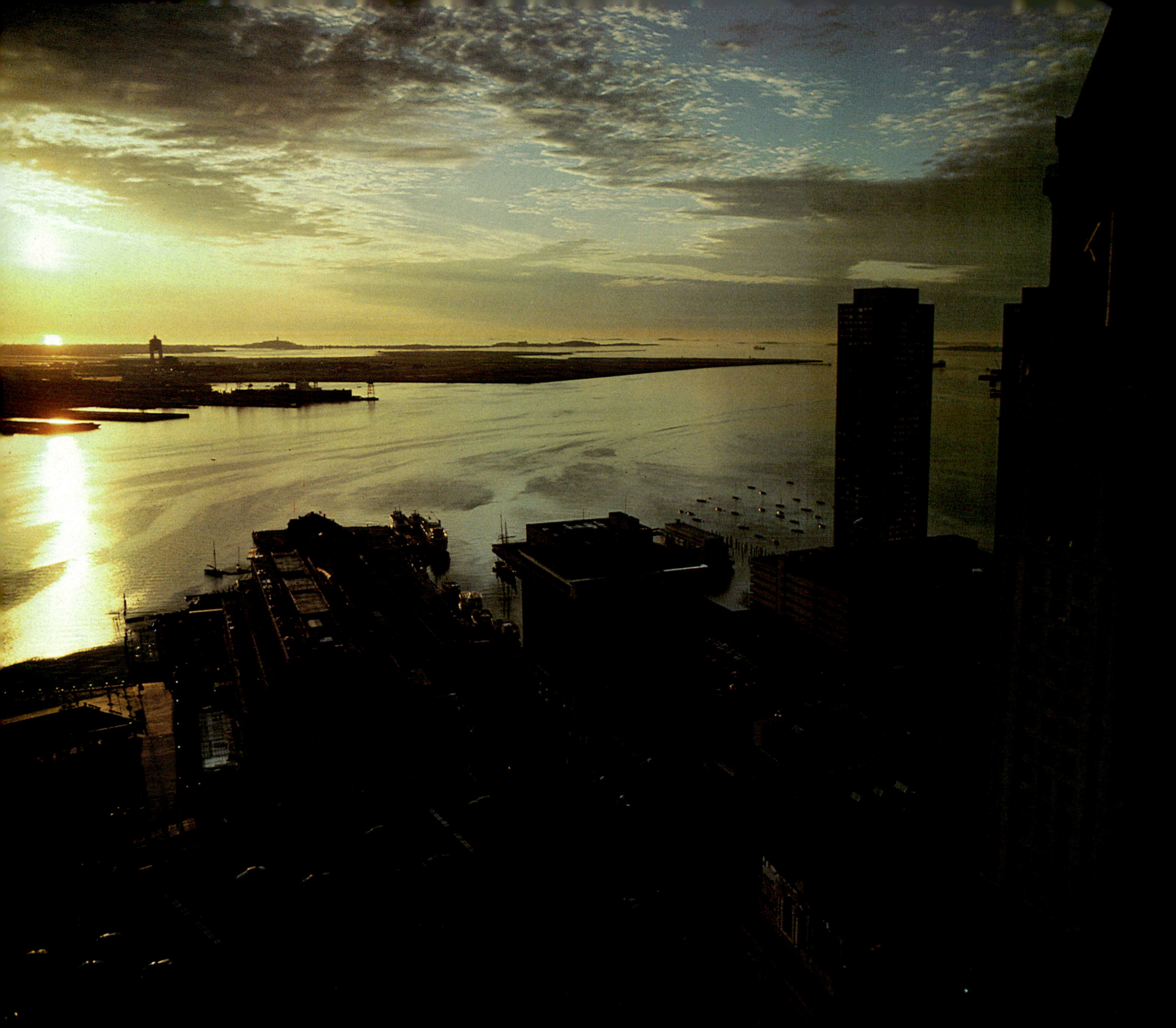

66 *(left)* The Custom House, Boston's first skyscraper, overlooks Boston Harbor.

67 Sunrise over Boston Harbor.

68 The Old Granary Burial Ground (1660). If you wander around you'll find the headstones of Paul Revere, Samuel Adams, John Hancock, Peter Faneuil and 'Mother Goose'.

69 *(right)* In operation since 1877, the Swan Boat is still one of Boston's most popular summer attractions.

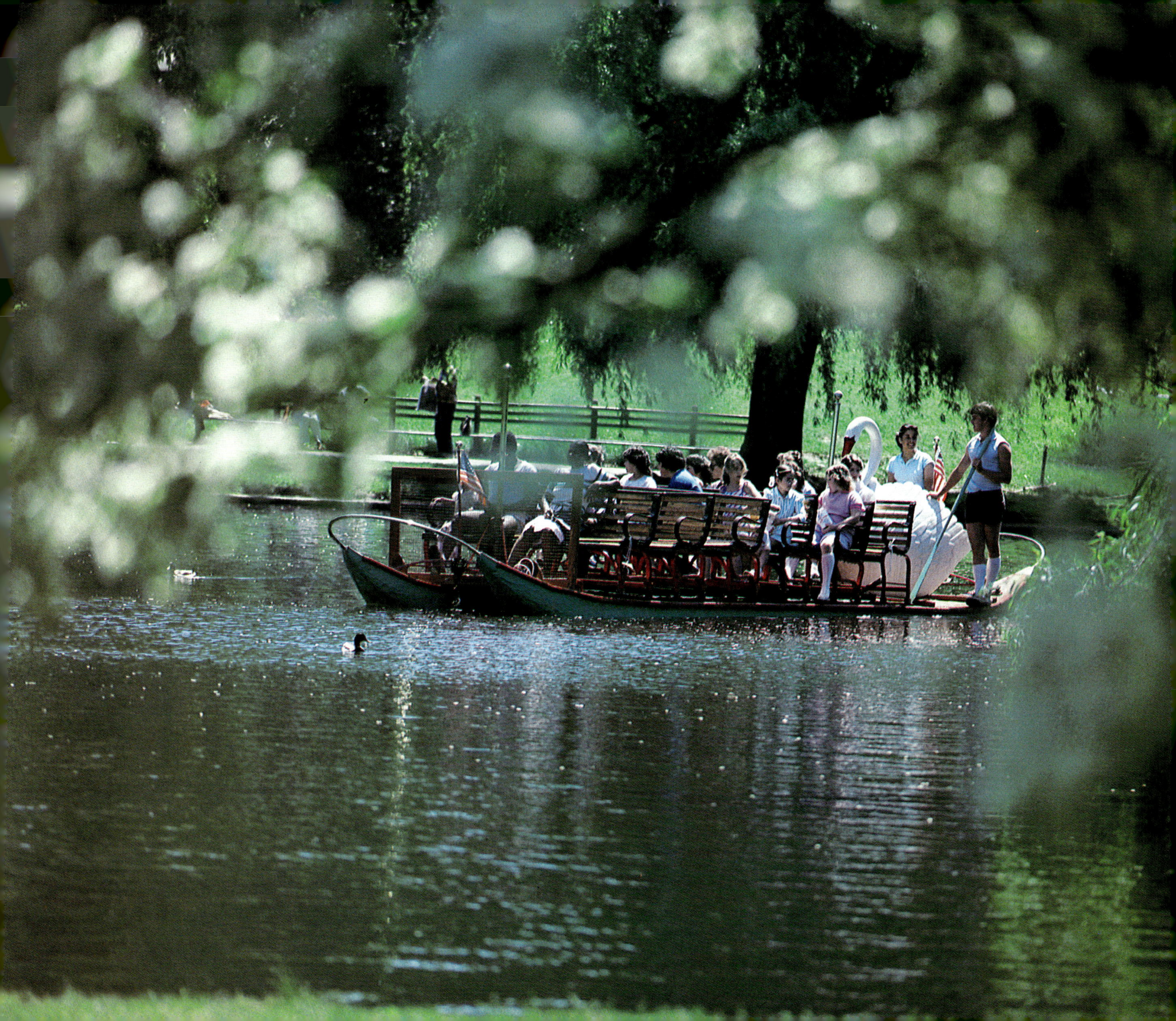

70 Various relics of Haymarket shoppers are cast in bronze and placed in the pavement.

71 This elegantly designed staircase is typical of the rich architectural quality found in Boston's more prominent structures.

The Pavilion Shops
OLD TOWN TROLLEY TOURS
TICKETS SOLD HERE

72 *(left)* The entrance to Copley Place connects two world-class hotels with several floors of internationally known shops and office space.

73 The garden islands along Commonwealth Avenue contain many historical monuments. This one is of John Glover from Marblehead. He was a soldier of the Revolution who commanded a regiment of a thousand men. In 1777 he was appointed a Brigadier General.

74 This interior of the King's Chapel shows the Governor's box. The chapel was the first Anglican church in Boston and the official church of the Crown.

75 The Old North Church was originally known as Christ Church and is the oldest standing church in Boston.

76 The 'Longfellow Room' where Longfellow was married (see 47) is now the residence of Mr. & Mrs. James Sullivan.

77 Many of the entrances of Boston residences display wrought ironwork. This one can be found on Mount Vernon Street on Beacon Hill.

78 The Senate Chamber is located directly below the gold dome of the State House. The sunburst design (Bulfinch) on the ceiling remains the same as the original. It is here that Massachusetts Senators sit in a circle and voting is done by voice. The public is allowed to sit in the galleries above.

79 Detail of The Old North Church Steeple where Paul Revere's lantern hung.

80 Celestial emanations from the dome at Quincy Market.

81 *(right)* A lone oarsman on the Charles River.

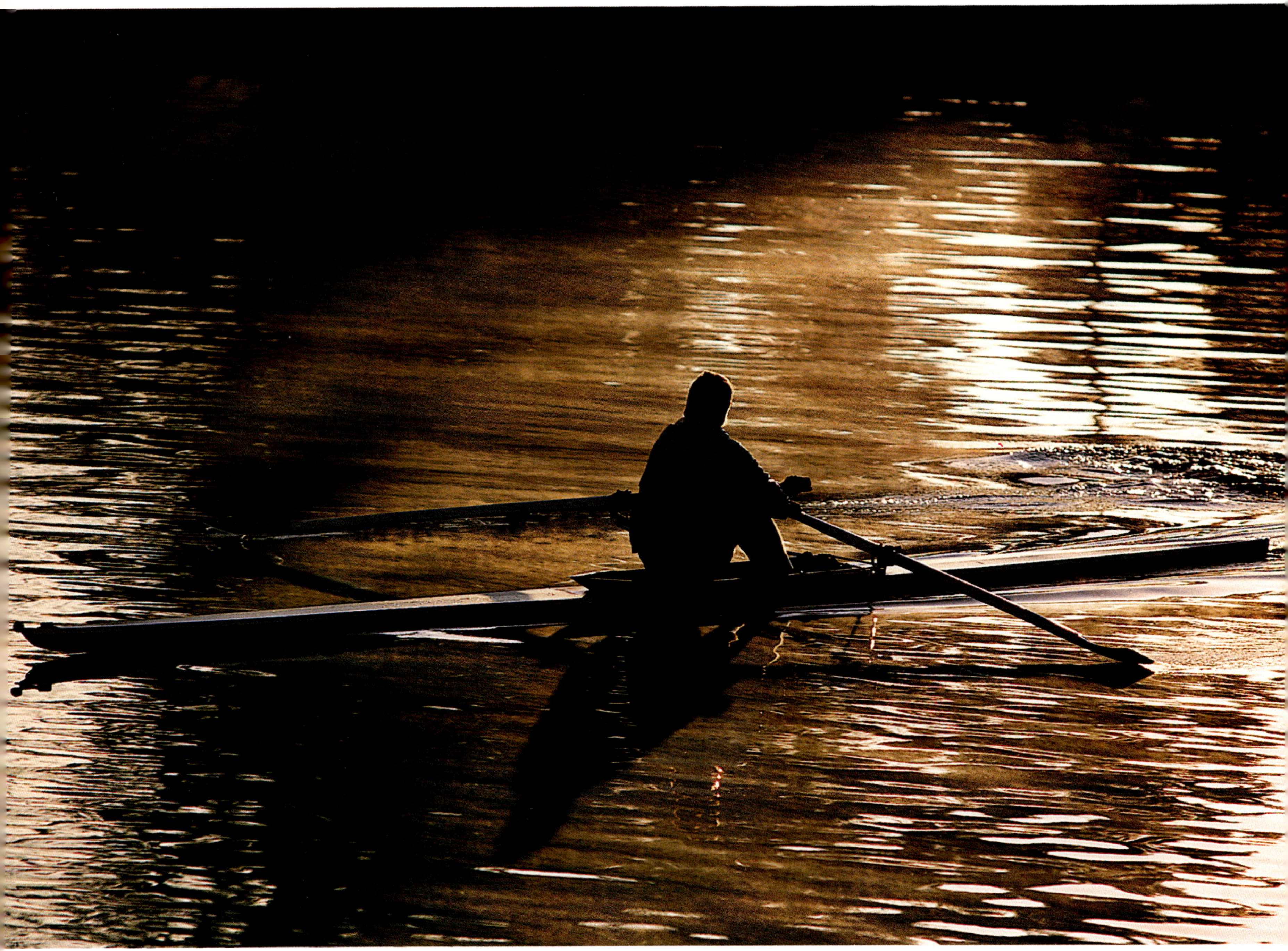

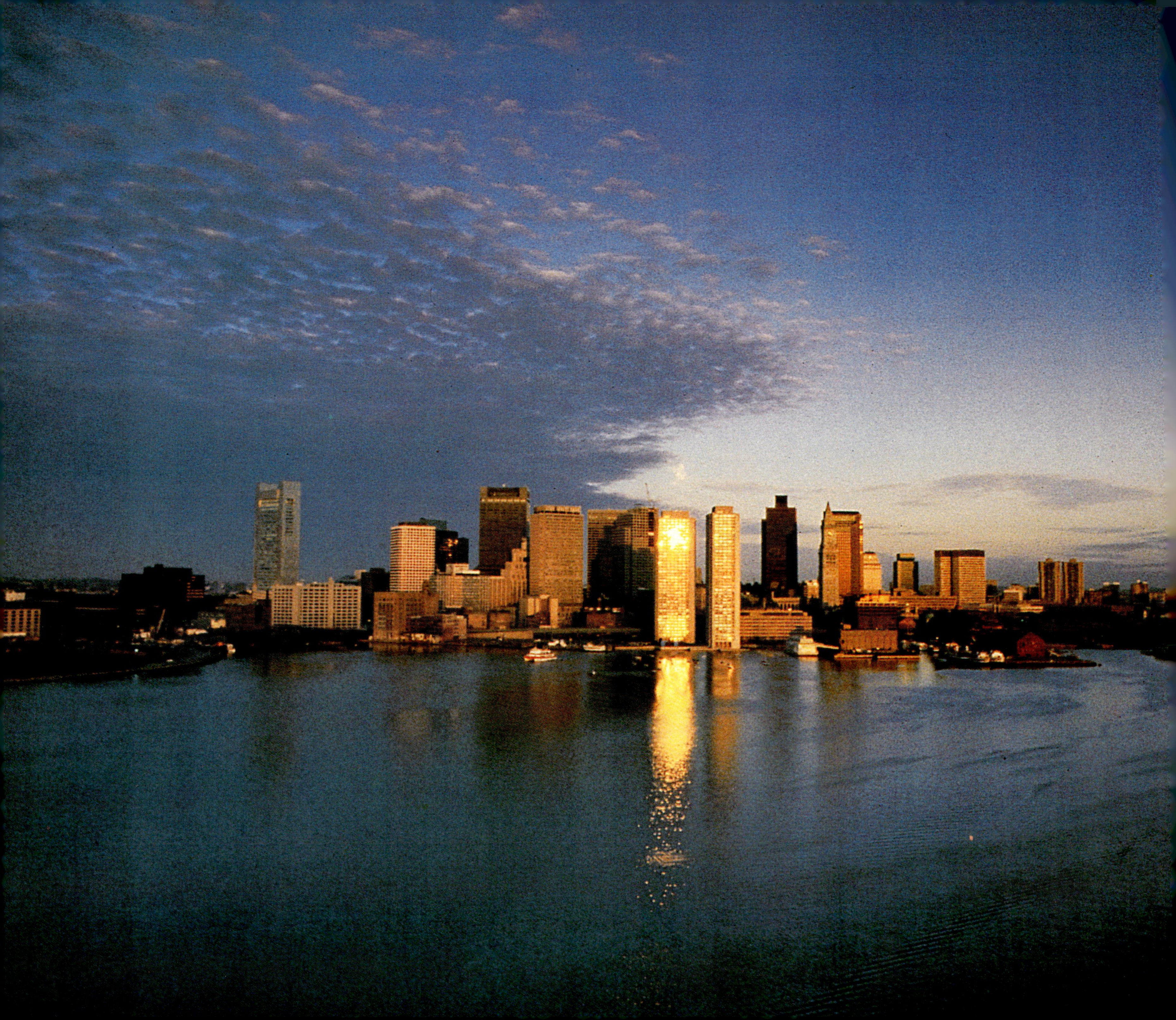

82 *(left)* A city on the water.

83 The harbor at daybreak.

84 Purple panes of glass appear in many of the windows on Beacon Hill. The early settlers brought it over as ballast in the bottom of their ships. This view from the Women's City Club looks out onto the Boston Common.

85 *(right)* Boston looks like a distant mythical city from the shoreline of Swampscott.

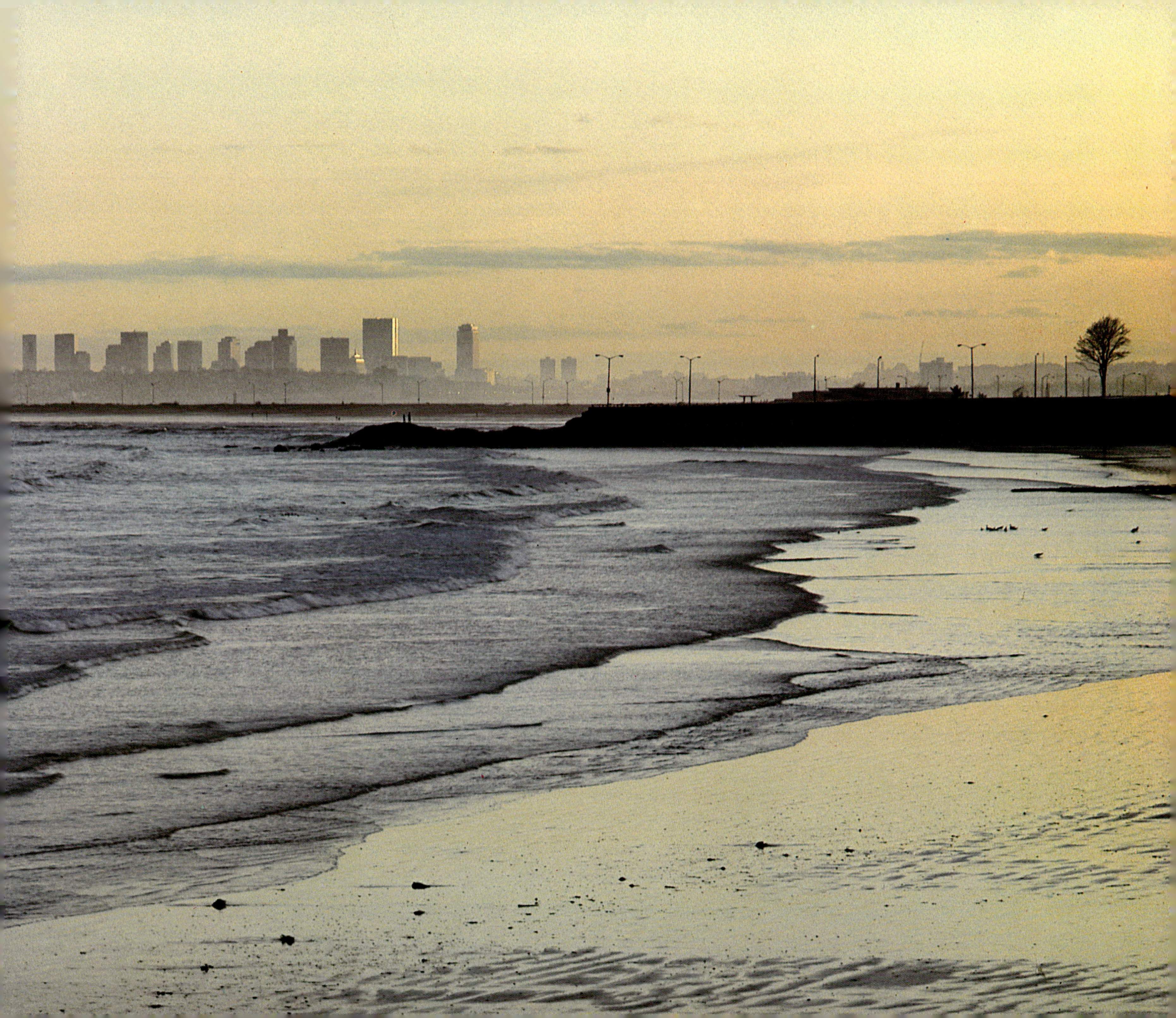

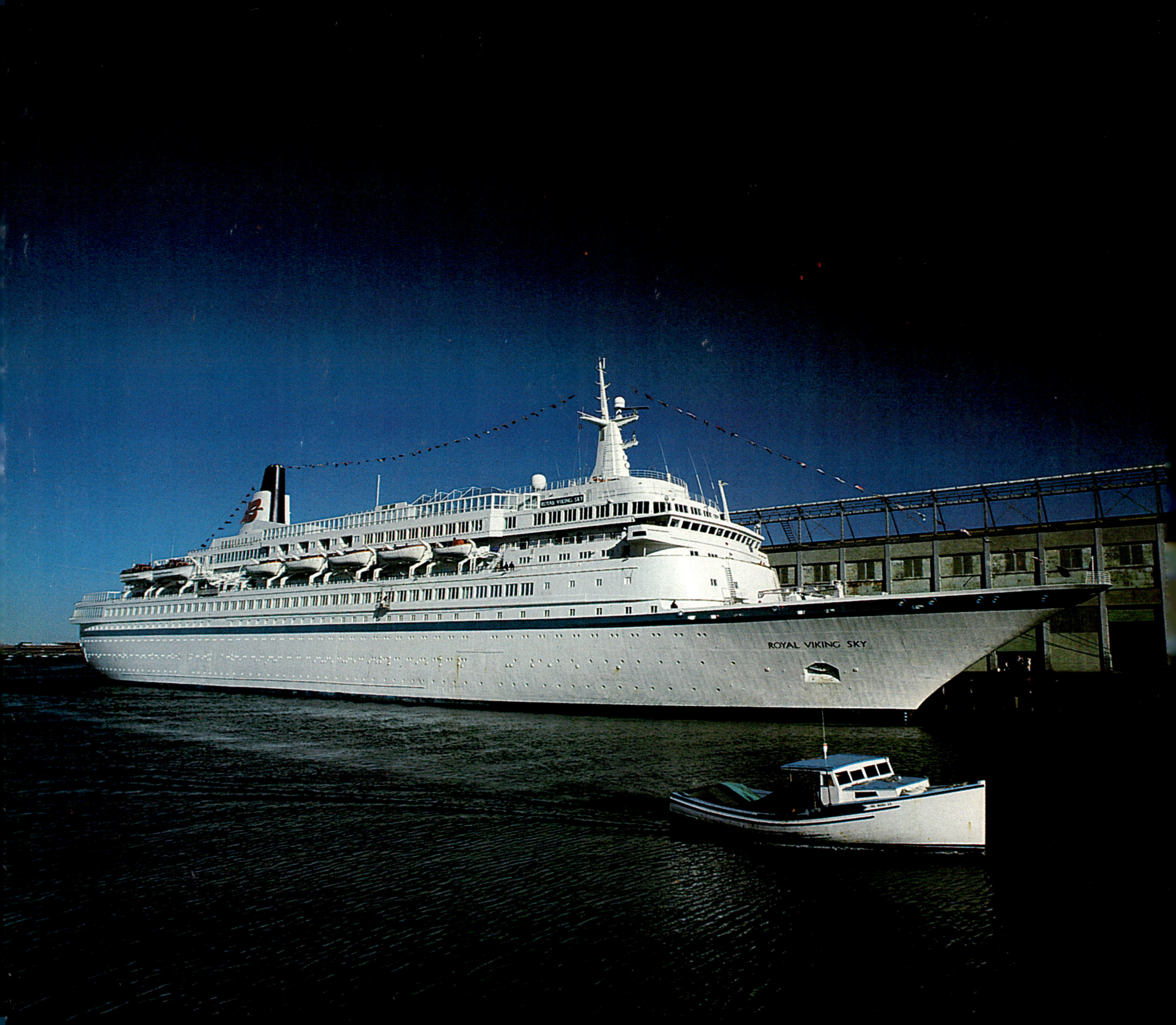
ROYAL VIKING SKY

86 *(left)* Large cruise ships make Boston a port-of-call.

87 Rush Hour.

88 Magnolia trees herald the arrival of Spring on Commonwealth Avenue.